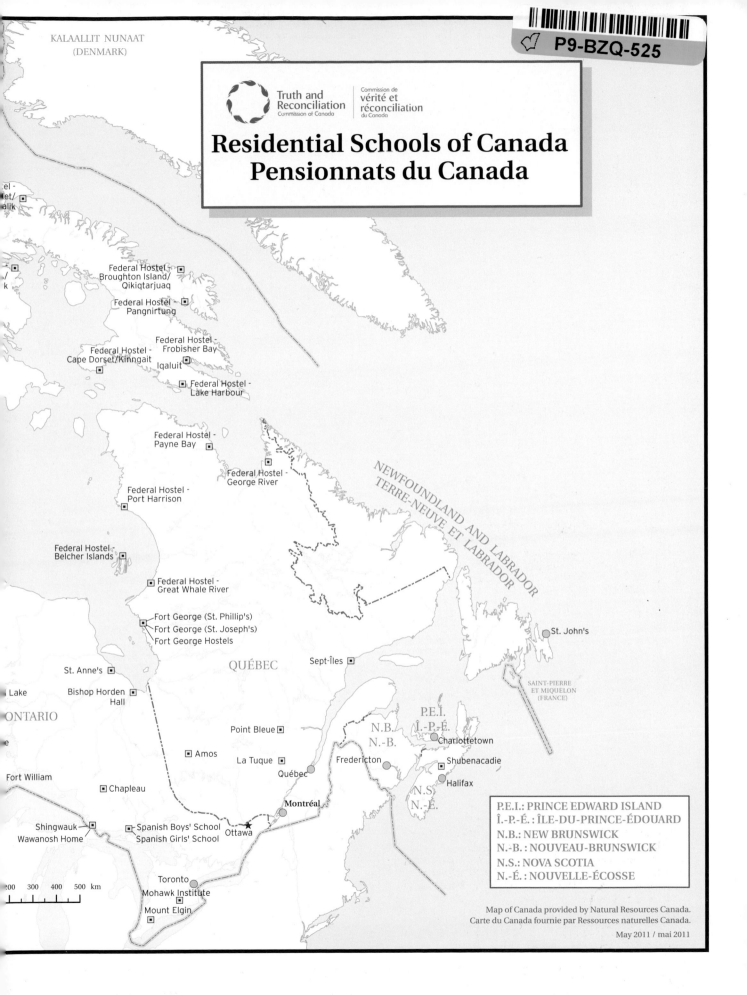

Residential Schools of Canada
Pensionnats du Canada

Truth and Reconciliation Commission of Canada
Commission de vérité et réconciliation du Canada

KALAALLIT NUNAAT
(DENMARK)

Federal Hostel -
Broughton Island/
Qikiqtarjuaq

Federal Hostel -
Pangnirtung

Federal Hostel -
Frobisher Bay

Federal Hostel -
Cape Dorset/Kinngait

Iqaluit

Federal Hostel -
Lake Harbour

Federal Hostel -
Payne Bay

Federal Hostel -
George River

Federal Hostel -
Port Harrison

Federal Hostel -
Belcher Islands

Federal Hostel -
Great Whale River

Fort George (St. Phillip's)
Fort George (St. Joseph's)
Fort George Hostels

NEWFOUNDLAND AND LABRADOR
TERRE-NEUVE ET LABRADOR

QUÉBEC

Sept-Îles

St. John's

SAINT-PIERRE
ET MIQUELON
(FRANCE)

St. Anne's

Bishop Horden
Hall

Lake

ONTARIO

Point Bleue

P.E.I.
Î.-P.-É.

N.B.
N.-B.

Charlottetown

Amos

La Tuque

Fredericton

Shubenacadie

Québec

Halifax

Fort William

Chapleau

Montréal

N.S.
N.-É.

Shingwauk
Wawanosh Home

Spanish Boys' School
Spanish Girls' School

Ottawa

Toronto
Mohawk Institute

Mount Elgin

P.E.I.: PRINCE EDWARD ISLAND
Î.-P.-É.: ÎLE-DU-PRINCE-ÉDOUARD
N.B.: NEW BRUNSWICK
N.-B.: NOUVEAU-BRUNSWICK
N.S.: NOVA SCOTIA
N.-É.: NOUVELLE-ÉCOSSE

200 300 400 500 km

Map of Canada provided by Natural Resources Canada.
Carte du Canada fournie par Ressources naturelles Canada.

May 2011 / mai 2011

*Back of map created by the Truth and Reconciliation Commission Of Canada

Residential Schools/Pensionnats	Location/Emplacement	Church/Église
Alberta		
Assumption (Hay Lakes)	Assumption	C
Blue Quills (Saddle Lake, Sacred Heart, Lac la Biche)	Lac la Biche, 1891-98 Saddle Lake, 1898-1931 St. Paul, 1931	C
Crowfoot (Blackfoot, St. Joseph's, St. Trinité)	Cluny	C
Desmarais (St. Martins, Wabiscaw Lake, Wabasca)	Desmarais-Wabasca	C
Edmonton (Red Deer Industrial, St. Albert)	St. Albert	U
Ermineskin	Hobbema	C
Fort Vermilion (St. Henry's)	Fort Vermillion	C
Grouard (St. Bernard's, Lesser Slave Lake Roman Catholic)	Grouard	C
Holy Angels (Fort Chipewyan, École des Saints-Anges)	Fort Chipewyan	C
Joussard (St. Bruno's)	Joussard	C
Lac la Biche (Notre Dame des Victoires, Blue Quills)	Lac La Biche	C
Lesser Slave Lake (St. Peter's)	Lesser Slave Lake	4A
Morley (Stony/Stoney)	Morley	U
Old Sun (Blackfoot)	Gleichen	A
Sacred Heart (Peigan, Brocket)	Brocket	C
St. Albert (Youville)	Youville	C
St. Augustine (Smoky River)	Peace River	C
St. Cyprian's (Victoria Home, Peigan)	Brocket	A
St. Joseph's (High River, Dunbow)	High River	C
St. Mary's (Blood, Immaculate Conception)	Cardston	C
St. Paul's (Blood)	Cardston	A
Sarcee (St. Barnabas)	Sarcee Junction, T'suu Tina	A
Sturgeon Lake (Calais, St. Francis Xavier)	Calais	C
Wabasca (St. John's)	Wabasca Lake	A
Whitefish Lake (St. Andrew's)	Whitefish Lake, Atikameg, (St. Andrew's Mission)	A
British Columbia / Colombie-Britannique		
Ahousat	Ahousat	U
Alberni	Port Alberni	U
Anahim (Anahim Lake)	Anahim Lake	N
Cariboo (St. Joseph's, William's Lake)	Williams Lake	C
Christie (Clayquot, Kakawis)	Tofino	C
Coqualeetza	Chilliwack	U
Cranbrook (St. Eugene's, Kootenay)	Cranbrook	C
Kamloops	Kamloops	C
Kitimaat	Kitimaat	U
Kuper Island	Kuper Island	C
Lejac (Fraser Lake)	Fraser Lake	C
Lower Post	Lower Post	C
Port Simpson (Crosby Home for Girls)	Port Simpson	A

Residential Schools/Pensionnats	Location/Emplacement	Church/Église
St. George's (Lytton)	Lytton	A
St. Mary's (Mission)	Mission	C
St. Michael's (Alert Bay Girls' Home, Alert Bay Boys' Home)	Alert Bay	A
St. Paul's (Squamish, North Vancouver)	North Vancouver	C
Sechelt	Sechelt	C
Manitoba		
Assiniboia (Winnipeg)	Winnipeg	C
Birtle	Birtle	P
Brandon	Brandon	U/C
Churchill Vocational Centre	Churchill	N
Cross Lake (St. Joseph's, Norway House, Jack River Annex, Notre Dame Hostel)	Cross Lake	C
Elkhorn (Washakada)	Elkhorn	A
Fort Alexander (Pine Falls)	Pine Falls	C
Guy Hill (Clearwater, The Pas, Sturgeon Landing (SK))	Clearwater Lake	C
Mackay - Dauphin	Dauphin	A
Mackay - The Pas	The Pas	A
Norway House	Norway House	U
Pine Creek (Camperville)	Camperville	C
Portage la Prairie	Portage la Prairie	U
Sandy Bay	Sandy Bay Reserve	C
Northwest Territories/Territoires du Nord-Ouest		
Akaitcho Hall (Yellowknife)	Yellowknife	N
Aklavik - Immaculate Conception	Aklavik	C
Aklavik (All Saints)	Aklavik	A
Federal Hostel - Fort Franklin	Déline	N
Fort McPherson (Fleming Hall)	Fort McPherson	A
Fort Providence (Sacred Heart)	Fort Providence	C
Fort Resolution (St. Joseph's)	Fort Resolution	C
Fort Simpson - Bompas Hall (Koe Go Cho)	Fort Simpson	A
Fort Simpson - Lapointe Hall (Deh Cho Hall, Koe Go Cho)	Fort Simpson	C
Fort Smith - Breynat Hall	Fort Smith	C
Fort Smith - Grandin College	Fort Smith	C
Hay River (St. Peter's)	Hay River	A
Inuvik - Grollier Hall	Inuvik	C
Inuvik - Stringer Hall	Inuvik	A
Nova Scotia / Nouvelle-Écosse		
Shubenacadie	Shubenacadie	C
Nunavut		
Chesterfield Inlet (Joseph Bernier, Turquetil Hall)	Chesterfield Inlet	C
Coppermine (Tent Hostel)	Coppermine	A
Federal Hostel - Baker Lake/Qamani'tuaq	Qamanittuaq	N

Residential Schools/Pensionnats	Location/Emplacement	Church/Église
Federal Hostel - Belcher Islands	South Camp, Flaherty Island	N
Federal Hostel - Broughton Island/Qikiqtarjuaq	Qikiqtarjuaq	N
Federal Hostel - Cambridge Bay	Cambridge Bay	N
Federal Hostel - Cape Dorset/Kinngait	Kinngait	N
Federal Hostel - Eskimo Point/Arviat	Arviat	N
Federal Hostel - Frobisher Bay (Ukkivik)	Iqaluit	N
Federal Hostel - Igloolik/Iglulik	Igloolik/Iglulik	N
Federal Hostel - Lake Harbour	Kimmirut	N
Federal Hostel - Pangnirtung (Pangnirtang)	Pangnirtung/Panniqtuuq	N
Federal Hostel - Pond Inlet/Mittimatalik	Mittimatalik	N

Ontario

Residential Schools/Pensionnats	Location/Emplacement	Church/Église
Bishop Horden Hall (Moose Fort, Moose Factory)	Moose Factory Island	A
Cecilia Jeffrey (Kenora, Shoal Lake)	Kenora	P
Chapleau (St. Joseph's, St. John's)	Chapleau	A
Cristal Lake		M
Fort Frances (St. Margaret's)	Fort Frances	C
Fort William (St. Joseph's)	Fort William	C
McIntosh (Kenora)	McIntosh	C
Mohawk Institute	Brantford	A
Mount Elgin (Muncey, St. Thomas)	Muncey	U
Pelican Lake (Pelican Falls)	Sioux Lookout	A
Poplar Hill	Poplar Hill	M
St. Anne's (Fort Albany)	Fort Albany	C
St. Mary's (Kenora, St. Anthony's)	Kenora	C
Shingwauk	Sault Ste. Marie	A
Spanish Boys' School (Charles Garnier, St. Joseph's, Wikwemikong Industrial)	Spanish	C
Spanish Girls' School (St. Joseph's, St. Peter's, St. Anne's, Wikwemikong Industrial)	Spanish	C
Stirland	Stirland	M

Québec

Residential Schools/Pensionnats	Location/Emplacement	Church/Église
Amos (St. Marc-de-Figuery)	Amos	C
Fort George (St. Phillip's)	Fort George	A
Fort George (St. Joseph's Mission, Residence Couture, Sainte-Thérèse-de-l'Enfant- Jésus)	Fort George	C
Federal Hostel - George River	Kangirsualujjuaq	N
Federal Hostel - Great Whale River (Poste-de-la-Baleine, Kuujjaraapik)	Kuujjuaraapik/ Whapmaguustui	N
Federal Hostel - Payne Bay (Bellin)	Kangirsuk	N
Federal Hostel - Port Harrison (Inoucdjouac, Innoucdouac)	Inukjuak	N
La Tuque	La Tuque	A
Point Bleue	Pointe-Bleue	C
Sept-Îles (Seven Islands, Notre Dame, Maliotenam)	Sept-Îles	C

Saskatchewan

Residential Schools/Pensionnats	Location/Emplacement	Church/Église
Battleford	Battleford	A
Beauval (Lac la Plonge)	Beauval	C
Cote Improved Federal Day School	Kamsack	U
Crowstand	Kamsack	P
File Hills	Balcarres	U
Fort Pelly	Fort Pelly	C
Gordon's Gordon's Reserve	Punnichy	A
Lac La Ronge	Lac La Ronge	A
Lebret (Qu'Appelle, Whitecalf, St. Paul's High School)	Lebret	C
Marieval (Cowesess, Crooked Lake)	Cowesess Reserve	C
Muscowequan (Lestock, Touchwood)	Lestock	C
Onion Lake	Onion Lake	A
Prince Albert (Onion Lake, St. Alban's, All Saints, St. Barnabas, Lac La Ronge)	Prince Albert	A
Regina	Regina	P
Round Lake	Broadview	U
St. Anthony's (Onion Lake, Sacred Heart)	Onion Lake	C
St. Michael's (Duck Lake)	Duck Lake	C
St. Phillip's	Kamsack	C
Sturgeon Landing (Guy Hill, Manitoba)	Sturgeon Landing	C
Thunderchild (Delmas, St. Henri)	Delmas	C

Yukon

Residential Schools/Pensionnats	Location/Emplacement	Church/Église
Carcross (Chooulta)	Carcross	A
Coudert Hall (Whitehorse Hostel/Student Residence, Yukon Hall)	Whitehorse	C
St. Paul's Hostel (Dawson City)	Dawson	A
Shingle Point (St. John's)	Shingle Point	A
Whitehorse Baptist (Lee Mission)	Whitehorse	B
Yukon Hall (Whitehorse/Protestant Hostel)	Whitehorse	N

Church / Église
A = Anglican / Anglicane
B = Baptist / Baptiste
C = Catholic / Catholique
M = Mennonite / Mennonite
N = Non-denominational / Non-confessionelle
P = Presbyterian / Presbytérienne
U = United / Unie

EVERY CHILD MATTERS®

2020 Official Orange Shirt
Designed by Jack Eiteneier

Orange Shirt Day began in 2013. I've always wanted to tell the story of how Orange Shirt Day started and to acknowledge the people who were involved in its creation. Thank you to everyone who continues to participate in Orange Shirt Day across Canada and beyond.

I didn't just get out of bed one day and decide that September 30th would be Orange Shirt Day. There is a story behind it, a long line of events that took place and people who contributed to making the day what it is today. Through this book I have the chance to tell my story and thank the people who have helped to create this movement.

Thank you for taking the time to read this book. I hope it will fill in some of the gaps to help you understand what Orange Shirt Day is all about; why the colour orange, why we chose the slogan "Every Child Matters", and the need to honour Residential School Survivors, their families, and to remember those children who didn't come home.
With respect and in friendship,

Phyllis Webstad

"Every Child Matters"

Project Manager: Teddy Anderson
Design: Eden Sunflower
Researcher and Content Editor : Brianna Shambrook
Proof Reading: Kaitlyn Stampflee
Text & illustration copyright © Medicine Wheel Education, Victoria, B.C., 2020
All rights reserved.
Printed in PRC
ISBN: 978-1-989122-43-3
For more book information go to www.orangeshirtday.org or
www.medicinewheel.education

Cover photo by Naomi Beliveau
Phyllis Webstad on cover photographed by Danielle Shack of DS Photography

Thank you

The Orange Shirt Society would like to thank all the wonderful people who, because of their sacrifice of time and energy, led to the creation of Orange Shirt Day and the Orange Shirt Society.

Without you, this movement would not be possible. Whether you were an artist, volunteer, Chief, government official, participant, sponsor, student, teacher, Survivor, member of a Survivor's family, current or past board member of the Orange Shirt Society or any other future participant, we would like to thank each of you for your contribution in making Orange Shirt Day what it is today.

Traditional Territory Acknowledgment

Medicine Wheel Education and the Orange Shirt Society acknowledge that this book was developed on the traditional territories of the Coast Salish peoples including the Sc'ianew people, the Lekwungen people, the T'Sou-ke people as well as on the traditional territories of the Interior Salish people, the Secwépemc (Shuswap), including the T'exelcemc First Nation (Williams Lake Indian Band) and the Xatśūll First Nation (Soda Creek Indian Band).

TABLE OF CONTENTS

INTRODUCTION
TO ORANGE SHIRT DAY

Welcome. Kukwstsetsélp (Thank you to all) for your courage and for opening your heart to learning, growing and striving to make our country more inclusive and unified. By reading Orange Shirt Day, you are embarking on an important journey to increase your knowledge and understanding of the significance of Orange Shirt Day, the Orange Shirt Society, Canada's shameful history of Indian Residential Schools, and their impacts, and **Indian Residential School Reconciliation.**

The only way to achieve Indian Residential School reconciliation is to acknowledge the true history and learn from it, no matter how difficult. The Orange Shirt Society hopes this book will help you to feel confident and empowered to continue to work towards Indian Residential School reconciliation regardless of your age, background and position in life. Everyone has a part to play. This book will further your understanding, and will guide you along your path of becoming a champion of Orange Shirt Day.

As you begin your journey in understanding Orange Shirt Day and reconciliation, we ask that you pay close attention to your heart, mind and feelings. If you feel sad or troubled while reading this book, please take a break and talk to a parent, teacher, or adult you trust about what you are feeling.

Indian Residential School Reconciliation is an ongoing collective process that involves both Indigenous and non-Indigenous Canadians bravely acknowledging, and educating each other, on the mistreatment of Indigenous peoples through the Residential School System. Reconciliation aims to create a new legacy for Indigenous Canadians that supports a healing journey and sees a respectful resurgence of cultural traditions.

CANADA BASED TOLL-FREE HELP LINES

- 24-hour National Indian Residential School crisis line at 1-866-925-4419
- First Nations and Inuit Mental Health and Wellness at 1-855-242-3310
- Kids Help Phone at 1-800-668-6868
- Suicide Prevention and Support at 1-833-456-4566
- 9-1-1 Emergency

This book was created to educate you on the Orange Shirt Day movement, Indian Residential School history and the process of reconciliation. There is something for everyone within these pages and it is our hope that as you read this book you will become educated and gain knowledge that you can pass on to other people. The Orange Shirt Society invites teachers, government officials, parents and other influential people to use this text as an educational tool and offer this knowledge to the younger generations who are forging new paths for a bright future.

TERMINOLOGY USED IN THIS BOOK

Indian is an erroneous and outdated term used to describe Indigenous people. It is based on the mistaken assumption by early European explorers that they had arrived in India. Unfortunately, it is still a *'legal'* term employed within the 1876 Indian Act, which is still in use. Today *'Indian'* is a derogatory term, and it will only be used in this book when referring to Indian Residential Schools and other legal terms within the Indian Act.[1]

Indigenous, or **Aboriginal**, people, *"are the descendants of the original inhabitants of North America. The Canadian Constitution recognizes three groups of Aboriginal people - Indians, Métis and Inuit. These are three separate peoples with unique heritages, languages, cultural practices and spiritual beliefs."* [2]

First Nations *"is a term used to describe Aboriginal peoples of Canada who are ethnically neither Métis nor Inuit."* [3]

Inuit *"Aboriginal people in Northern Canada, who live in Nunavut, Northwest Territories, Northern Quebec and Northern Labrador. The word means 'people' in the Inuit language —Inuktitut. The singular of Inuit is Inuk."* [4]

Métis people are *"...mixed First Nation and European ancestry who identify themselves as Métis, as distinct from First Nations people, Inuit or non-Aboriginal people."* [5]

WHAT THIS BOOK EXPLORES

Orange Shirt Day, September 30th, is a day to honour Residential School Survivors, their families, and remember those **children who didn't come home**. This book will provide you with an opportunity to understand the power and significance of reconciliation in regards to Orange Shirt Day. It is everyone's responsibility to understand the continuing impacts connected to this **National trauma** and how we all, as people of varying backgrounds, ancestry and age, can ensure Residential Schools never happen again. In order to embrace reconciliation and change all of us, both Indigenous and non-Indigenous, must come together to promote the healing and acknowledgment of this tragic time in Canadian history. Everyone must work together for a better and inclusive future in which EVERY CHILD MATTERS.

Chief Willie Sellars, Elder Millie Emile, Elder Virginia Gilbert and Phyllis Webstad at the 2019 Williams Lake Orange Shirt Day. Photo is by Monica Lamb-Yorski of the Williams Lake Tribune.

Children who didn't come home from Residential Schools because they died, from malnutrition, disease or injuries due to the circumstances and abuses endured at the schools. Many children also attempted to run away from the Residential Schools, but they died trying to find their way home. Records show that 6000 children died in Residential Schools, but the records are incomplete and it is believed that far more children didn't come home. [6]

A **National trauma** occurs when a traumatic event or experience affects a collective group of people across a country. Indian Residential Schools have resulted in a national trauma.

The City of **Williams Lake** lies within the Cariboo Regional District of British Columbia and is situated on the traditional territory of the T'exelcemc (Williams Lake Band People), who are members of the Secwépemc Nation (Shuswap People). [7]

THE BOOK AT A GLANCE

- A brief history of the events leading to the implementation of Residential Schools
- A brief history of Residential Schools in Canada, focusing on the impacts of St. Joseph's Mission Residential School in **Williams Lake**, B.C.
- The St. Joseph's Mission Residential School Commemoration Project started a vision of reconciliation that led to Orange Shirt Day
- The creation and movement of Orange Shirt Day and the Orange Shirt Society
- How to participate in Orange Shirt Day respectfully, authentically and effectively
- Reflections on Reconciliation
- Student art submissions from Canada exploring reconciliation and Orange Shirt Day

This book will feature student art projects inspired by Orange Shirt Day. These art pieces are reflections of the thought processes of students across Canada in response to the Orange Shirt Day movement. The Orange Shirt Society sincerely thanks the hundreds of brilliant students and teachers who kindly submitted their artwork. Although not every art piece could be included, the Orange Shirt Society is humbled by the amazing and creative responses. Chapter 8 is devoted to student art pieces. See page 133.

Terms that require a definition will be shown in **bold font**. For these terms, there will be a definition provided at the bottom of the text and/or in the back of the book in the glossary.

To engage with this book effectively as a teacher, there is an educational curriculum-based study guide designed to give additional tools and resources specialized for the classroom. For more information please visit
www.medicinewheel.education/orangeshirtday.

For more Orange Shirt Day resources visit **www.orangeshirtsociety.org**

Photo is by Jacqueline Maurer. These orange medicine pouches were crafted by the Dze L K'ant Friendship Centre on the Wet'suwet'en Territory.

INTRODUCTION QUESTIONS

REVIEW

1. What is Indian Residential School Reconciliation?

2. How can we achieve Indian Residential School Reconciliation?

3. Define the term Indian. In what context is that term acceptable and in what context is it derogatory?

4. Define the term Indigenous people or Aboriginal people.

5. What is the appropriate term for the Indigenous people from Northern Canada, who live in Nunavut, Northwest Territories, Northern Quebec and Northern Labrador?

6. This word means "people" in the Inuktitut language.

7. Define Métis. Who are they?

8. According to the text, how many children died because of the Residential School System and were never able to return to their homes?

9. Whose traditional territory is Williams Lake located on? What province is Williams Lake located in?

REFLECT

Why do you think it is important to use the correct term when referring to different Indigenous groups?

Why do we no longer use the term 'Indian' when speaking about Indigenous people?

SOURCES

1. "Indian." The Canadian Encyclopedia. May 11, 2020. <https://thecanadianencyclopedia.ca/en/article/indian-term> accessed May 15, 2020.
2. "Archived - Common Terminology." Indigenous and Northern Affairs Canada. March 11, 2013. <https://www.aadnc-aandc.gc.ca/eng/1358879361384/1358879407462> accessed May 1, 2020.
3. "Terminology." Indigenous Foundations UBC Arts. <https://indigenousfoundations.arts.ubc.ca/terminology/#firstnations> accessed May 1, 2020.
4. "Archived - Common Terminology." Indigenous and Northern Affairs Canada. March 11, 2013. <https://www.aadnc-aandc.gc.ca/eng/1358879361384/1358879407462> accessed May 1, 2020.
5. "Archived - Common Terminology." Indigenous and Northern Affairs Canada. March 11, 2013. <https://www.aadnc-aandc.gc.ca/eng/1358879361384/1358879407462> accessed May 1, 2020.
6. "Truth and Reconciliation Commission: By the numbers." CBC News. Daniel Schwartz. June 3, 2015. <https://www.cbc.ca/news/indigenous/truth-and-reconciliation-commission-by-the-numbers-1.3096185> accessed May 1, 2020.

   "Residential Schools Findings Point to 'Cultural Genocide,' commission chair says." CBC News. John Paul Tasker. May 15, 2015. <https://www.cbc.ca/news/politics/residential-schools-findings-point-to-cultural-genocide-commission-chair-says-1.3093580> accessed March 30, 2020.
7. Williams Lake Band. <https://williamslakeband.ca/> accessed April 30, 2020.

CHAPTER 1 THE VISION THAT
INSPIRED ORANGE SHIRT DAY

Orange Shirt Day, which takes place annually across Canada and beyond on September 30th, is a legacy of the St. Joseph's Mission Residential School Commemoration Project held in Williams Lake, B.C., in May of 2013. That week-long commemoration project was inspired by **Chief Fred Robbins**, who is Northern Secwépemc (Shuswap) from Esk'etemc First Nation (Alkali Lake).[1] Chief Fred Robbins had a vision for reconciliation which involved all people remembering and learning what happened at St. Joseph's Mission Residential School, honouring and helping the Survivors to recover from their experiences and ultimately reconciling together.

Chief Fred Robbins' vision was to create positive long-lasting change and harmony among Indigenous and non-Indigenous peoples within Williams Lake and throughout the Cariboo Region. In order to achieve this, he needed to involve the entire community in understanding and learning what happened in that Residential School just down the road, before any healing and reconciliation could take place.

In his efforts to bring people together, he invited Chiefs, Councils, local and provincial elected officials, RCMP officers, schools and churches, as well as Indigenous and non-Indigenous local residents to a series of community-building events.

CHIEF FRED ROBBINS

"

Every Child Matters. It's that next generation that we have to start teaching... We need to start creating a new legacy, and it starts within the communities... The people need to start coming together... Everything that ever happened to First Nations people across Canada started with these schools. Physical, sexual, mental, discrimination, genocide, treason, everything started with these schools. And to move forward we need to recognize that and that's why we are here today. Let's recognize that together as a people, not as First Nations and non-First Nations but as a people... that's how we have to do this.

"

- Chief Fred Robbins, Esk'etemc First Nation, May 17, 2013. [2]

Chief Fred Robbins photographed by John Dell.

Truth and Reconciliation
Commission of Canada

The Truth and Reconciliation Commission of Canada (TRC) was founded on June 2, 2008 and aimed to reveal the truths of Residential Schools and provide support for Survivors and their families. The TRC was created out of the Indian Residential School Settlement Agreement (IRSSA), which was announced in 2006. The IRSSA was an agreement between both the Government of Canada and Residential School Survivors. This agreement was reached to settle a class action lawsuit by Indian Residential School Survivors. It required that the Government of Canada issue an official apology and provide a compensation package of nearly two billion dollars that was paid out to Survivors.[3] At the time, it was recognized as the largest class action suit in Canadian history.

As a result of this historic settlement agreement, the TRC was created and the Government of Canada issued an official apology for its role in creating government-sponsored Residential Schools. On June 11, 2008, just days after the birth of the TRC, Prime Minister Stephen Harper stood in the House of Commons and issued an apology on behalf of Canada to all Residential School Survivors. [4]

Between 2008 and 2015, the TRC revealed the dark truths of Residential Schools and provided a platform for Indigenous peoples to be heard and begin their journey of reconciliation.

In order to effectively participate in the ongoing process of reconciliation, in its conclusion in 2015, the TRC offered 94 calls to action. The calls to action provide concrete steps on an array of reconciliation topics including education, child welfare, language and culture, health, and professional development. [5]

In 2013, the TRC travelled to Williams Lake to participate in the St. Joseph's Mission Commemoration Project events which were inspired by Chief Fred Robbins' vision for reconciliation. The TRC Chair, Chief Justice Murray Sinclair, who is now a Canadian Senator, participated in and chaired the events. The series of events included the unveiling of memorial monuments, a youth video project, educational opportunities, Survivor statement gathering and a reunion for Survivors. It was at these events that Phyllis Webstad shared the story of her orange shirt resulting in the international movement Orange Shirt Day. [6]

Chief Fred Robbins discusses reconciliation at a TRC event. Photo taken by John Dell.

CANADA'S APOLOGY

On June 11, 2008, former Prime Minister Stephen Harper issued a public apology for the role that the Canadian Government played in the Residential School System. Harper stood in the House of Commons and apologized. Here are some excerpts of that apology: [7]

"Mr. Speaker, I stand before you today to offer an apology to former students of Indian Residential Schools. The treatment of children in Indian Residential Schools is a sad chapter in our history. In the 1870s, the federal government, partly in order to meet its obligation to educate Aboriginal children, began to play a role in the development and administration of these schools.

...These objectives were based on the assumption Aboriginal cultures and spiritual beliefs were inferior and unequal. Indeed, some sought, as it was infamously said, `to kill the Indian in the child.' Today, we recognize that this policy of assimilation was wrong, has caused great harm, and has no place in our country.

...The Government of Canada built an educational system in which very young children were often forcibly removed from their homes, often taken far from their communities. Many were inadequately fed, clothed and housed. All were deprived of the care and nurturing of their parents, grandparents and communities. First Nations, Inuit and Métis languages and cultural practices were prohibited in these schools.

...It has taken extraordinary courage for the thousands of Survivors that have come forward to speak publicly about the abuse they suffered.

...It is a testament to their resilience as individuals and to the strength of their cultures. Regrettably, many former students are not with us today and died never having received a full apology from the Government of Canada.

...Therefore, on behalf of the Government of Canada and all Canadians, I stand before you, in this chamber so central to our life as a country, to apologize to Aboriginal Peoples for Canada's role in the Indian Residential Schools System.

...To the approximately 80,000 living former students, and all family members and communities, the Government of Canada now recognizes that it was wrong to forcibly remove children from their homes and we apologize for having done this.

...We now recognize that it was wrong to separate children from rich and vibrant cultures and traditions, that it created a void in many lives and communities, and we apologize for having done this.

...There is no place in Canada for the attitudes that inspired the Indian Residential Schools System to ever again prevail."

ROYAL CANADIAN MOUNTED POLICE APOLOGY

During the operation of Indian Residential Schools, the RCMP assisted Indian Agents and the Department of Indian Affairs with various requests such as finding and returning students who had run away from school. Ultimately, the RCMP were used as a tool by the government to maintain the system.

In May of 2004, former RCMP Commissioner Giuliano Zaccardelli issued a public apology on behalf of the RCMP. He said,

"...To those of you who suffered tragedies at Residential Schools, we are very sorry for your experience. Canadians can never forget what happened and they never should. The RCMP is optimistic that we can all work together to learn from this Residential School system experience and ensure that it never happens again. We - I, as Commissioner of the RCMP - am truly sorry for what role we played in the Residential School system and the abuse that took place in that system." [8]

Another apology was issued at a TRC event in March 2014 by another former RCMP Commissioner Bob Paulson. He said, *"... I say to you all here today, as Commissioner of the RCMP, on behalf of the RCMP and on behalf of all men and women who comprise the RCMP or have ever been a part of it, I am deeply sorry for what has happened to you and the part my organization played in it."* [9]

In 2011, the RCMP released a 470-page assessment that aimed to *"explain how police officers were linked with the school system and what actions the police took, if any, if they were aware of abuse."* [10] The assessment, which included thorough research and investigation efforts, is a testament to the RCMP's dedication to the healing and reconciliation process. *"This report helps prepare for the future as it permits assessment of past practices, actions and accomplishments, and provides an occasion for the RCMP to improve future ones."* [11]

PHYLLIS (JACK) WEBSTAD'S STORY

Phyllis Webstad photographed by Danielle Shack of DS Photography

A teepee set up for Orange Shirt Day 2015 in Calling Lake, Alberta. Photo taken by Angela Lightning.

Beadwork and photo by Kristin Spray.

In 2013, Residential School Survivor **Phyllis Webstad** was asked to speak at a press conference promoting reconciliation events in her community. Phyllis courageously shared her personal and traumatic experience. [12] Orange Shirt Day was born out of that speech. The influential efforts of Chief Fred Robbins, and later Phyllis Webstad, as well as many other people's efforts, led to the Orange Shirt Day movement. Now, Orange Shirt Day passionately spreads the message that "Every Child Matters."

Phyllis Webstad is Northern Secwépmc from Stswecem'c Xgat'tem First Nation, (Canoe Creek/Dog Creek Indian Band). When she was just six-years-old in 1973, she went to Residential School for the first time. On her first day at St. Joseph's Mission Residential School, near Williams Lake, B.C., she wore her brand new shiny orange shirt, bought for her by her Granny. Phyllis was so excited to go to school and wear her new shirt, but when she arrived her orange shirt was taken away, never to be worn again. She survived the Mission for 300 sleeps.

The orange shirt has now become a symbol of hope and reconciliation. To Phyllis, the colour orange has always symbolized that she did not matter. Today she has learned to accept the colour and even have fun with it. It also represents hope that Indigenous families and communities are healing, and it has become a symbol of defiance and commitment to a better future. By wearing an orange shirt on Orange Shirt Day, you are making a statement that Residential Schools were wrong and that you commit to the concept that
EVERY CHILD MATTERS.

Artwork by grade 7 student Abby Billard from Harold Peterson Middle School.

THIS IS PHYLLIS'S MESSAGE TO YOU

 Phyllis (Jack) Webstad

Dear Reader,

It seems like from the very beginning that this whole "Orange Shirt Movement" has been divinely guided. For whatever reason, I was chosen to do this work, whether I was ready or not. Things just happened without a lot of trying on my part. People, places and events just fell into place. I've often wondered why me? As soon as I'd think why me, I would tell myself - Why not me? When I was putting together my presentation for speaking and wondering about why my story is so accepted, I thought about it and came up with this:

Why is my story so accepted?

- Children – easy to understand.
- Non-First Nation people – can associate.
- Residential School Survivors and their families –also their story.
- It opens the door to discussion, in a gentle way, about a heavy topic.
- It is time.

My story is easy for children to understand. They can associate with shopping for going back to school, how exciting that is. They can then empathize with how it would feel to have someone take something away that their parents bought for their first day of school.

Non-Indigenous people have children, grandchildren, nieces, nephews. They can empathize and think of what it would feel like to have their children suddenly snatched from their homes and arms and be absolutely helpless to do anything about it. They cannot imagine!

My story is not unique, Residential School Survivors and their families can associate with my orange shirt story. Residential Schools happened in Canada from top to bottom, left to right. There are many stories (truths) that need to be and are being told. Families of Survivors are finding out why their lives are the way they are after understanding what their parents or grand-parents had to live through and how that experience is impacting their lives.

The topic of Residential Schools isn't pleasant. I offer my story in a gentle way as a conversation starter, a door opener to discussion about all aspects of Indian Residential School.

And lastly, it is time. It is time our truths be heard. It's time that non-Indigenous Canadians know the history of Indian Residential Schools. The Truth and Reconciliation Commission went across Canada and was wrapping up its tour in 2013 when they came to Williams Lake, B.C. Canadians were ready to keep the conversation happening after the TRC wrapped up.

I pledge to continue to do my best to be the face of the Orange Shirt movement. I've already met so many amazing people on my travels across Canada and I've come to witness and realize that our future is in good hands. The children in elementary and high schools get it, they are the generation that will change our society for the better and make sure that this never happens again.

I thank everyone that participates and wears an orange shirt on Orange Shirt Day, or any day of the year. By wearing an orange shirt, that means you care about what happened to us and that you are taking the time to learn. To us Survivors, it is a little bit of justice in our lifetime for what happened to us. We won't be around forever, one day there will be no Survivors left in Canada. My hope is Orange Shirt Day will continue to be the vehicle in telling the history long after we are gone.

Thank you for taking the time to learn about my story and about Orange Shirt Day. Please know that I do spend countless hours online looking at pictures, watching videos and reading about what you all are doing. I've always been a person who needs to know everything, it's taken me a while to comprehend that I will never know everything that is happening for Orange Shirt Day. So Kukstemcw, thank you, keep doing what you're doing.

I want to finish my message to you by saying that I do not claim to represent or speak for other Survivors or their families. I share my story and my family's story, which does not represent all other people's thoughts, experiences or perspectives.

All My Relations.

Phyllis W.

ORANGE SHIRT SOCIETY

The **Orange Shirt Society** is a non-profit organization, based in Williams Lake, B.C., which grew out of the events in 2013, inspired by Chief Fred Robbins' vision for reconciliation. The Orange Shirt Society board is composed of diverse members dedicated to raising awareness of the Residential Schools and supporting the development of Orange Shirt Day.

The Society's purposes: [13]

1.) To support Indian Residential School Reconciliation

2.) To create awareness of the individual, family and community intergenerational impacts of Indian Residential Schools though Orange Shirt Society activities

3.) To create awareness of the concept of "Every Child Matters"

Orange Shirt Society

Phyllis Webstad and the Orange Shirt Society are proud to have the opportunity to be involved in this project. Since 2013 the Society has worked hard to realize its purposes of bringing awareness to Canadians about Residential School impacts, to support Residential School impact awareness efforts across the country and to ensure that there is an understanding that the impact of Residential School is still present in our youth and that every child is important and matters and requires support to deal with the intergenerational impacts of Residential Schooling.

There is still a long way to go in the journey to reconciliation. The small role that Phyllis and the Orange Shirt Society play is to provide the opportunity for families, schools, businesses and organizations, as well as communities to involve themselves in the reconciliation journey, to learn more about what happened in the past and to translate that into what we can do in the present and future to reach reconciliation together.

Each year for the Orange Shirt Society, these efforts begin with the support of events across the country on September 30th, Orange Shirt Day. From there, the support continues throughout the rest of the year with presentations in schools, communities, organizations and businesses to get people thinking about and acting on reconciliation.

This book is part of the efforts to widen the conversation and action about reconciliation. Phyllis and the Orange Shirt Society are proud to be involved in this publication and hope that it will be of help across the country as people continue to work towards reconciliation.

Jerome Beauchamp
President of Orange Shirt Society

CHAPTER ONE QUESTIONS

REVIEW

1. Who is Chief Fred Robbins and where is he from?
2. What was Chief Fred Robbins' vision? Who did it include?
3. When was the Truth and Reconciliation Commission founded?
4. What was the goal of the Truth and Reconciliation Commission?
5. Who is Stephen Harper and what did he apologize for on June 11th, 2008?
6. Where did Canada's apology to Indigenous people for Residential Schools take place?
7. Who is Phyllis Webstad? Where is Phyllis Webstad from?
8. How old was Phyllis Webstad when she went to Residential School?
9. Where did Phyllis Webstad get her orange shirt from?
10. Did Phyllis Webstad ever get her shirt back?
11. Why do you think orange is the chosen colour of shirt for this commemorative day?
12. What is the Orange Shirt Society?
13 What is the central message of the Orange Shirt Society?

ACTIVITY

Phyllis Webstad wrote you a letter to encourage and thank you for taking the time to read this book, learn about Orange Shirt Day and participate in reconciliation. Now it's your turn. Write a letter to Phyllis Webstad. You may consider asking Phyllis questions or sharing your thoughts.

As someone whos never faced discrimination based on my skin tone and history, its hard to fully understand how this must feel for Indignous people. I've never had to go through this sort of suffering before but people of my colour have inflicted this pain on people countless times. It's important to me that we end the cycle of suffering for these people though I think many of these people will never get to feel free of those feelings and it upsets me that I can't do anything about that. But, growing up as someone whos part of the LGBT+ community, I understand why they would not be able to forgive and move on and Im not bothered by them feeling this way as we cannot fix all the suffering that has happened or will continue to happen. We can only truely teach love and acceptace to ourselves for the future.

REFLECT

1. The Truth and Reconciliation Commission of Canada (TRC) provided 94 Calls to Action to implement change in Canada. Why do you think the TRC used words such as "calls to action" vs suggestions? Reflect on the difference between these words and their impacts.

2. In Phyllis Webstad's letter to you, the reader, she says *"by wearing an orange shirt, what that means is that you care about what happened to us and that you are taking the time to learn. To us Survivors, it is a little bit of justice in our lifetime for what happened to us."* Why do you think Phyllis says "a little bit of justice" instead of "complete justice"? Do you think it is possible to have complete justice for what happened to Indigenous people?

3. Why do you think the Orange Shirt Society and Phyllis Webstad teach us the phrase "Every Child Matters"? Why do you think the Orange Shirt Society uses the phrase "Every Child Matters" and which children are they referring to?

RESEARCH

Stephen Harper apologized in 2008 for the Canadian Government's role in Residential Schools. Find the transcript of the apology. Why do you think the Canadian Government chose this time in history to issue an official apology for Residential Schools?

SOURCES

1. Tarbell, Harold. St. Joseph's Mission Residential School Commemoration Project Document. Remembering, Recovering, and Reconciling. Williams Lake: Tarbell Facilitation Network, 2013.
2. "Chief Fred Robbins Speech." Boitanio Park Monument Unveiling. The Commemoration Project Events. Filmed by John Dell. Signal Point Media, 2013. DVD.
3. "A Timeline of Residential Schools, the Truth and Reconciliation Commission." CBC News. May 16, 2008. < https://www.cbc.ca/news/canada/a-timeline-of-residential-schools-the-truth-and-reconciliation-commission-1.724434> accessed December. 1, 2019.
4. "Government Apology to Former Students of Indian Residential Schools." The Canadian Encyclopedia. April 15, 2015. <https://thecanadianencyclopedia.ca/en/article/government-apology-to-former-students-of-indian-residential-schools> accessed April 30, 2020.

   "Residential School." Truth and Reconciliation Commission. <http://www.trc.ca/about-us.html> accessed October 15, 2019.
5. "Truth and Reconciliation Commission of Canada: Calls to Action. Truth and Reconciliation Commission of Canada. 2015. <http://trc.ca/assets/pdf/Calls_to_Action_English2.pdf> accessed February 1, 2020.
6. Tarbell, Harold. St. Joseph's Mission Residential School Commemoration Project Document. Remembering, Recovering, and Reconciling. Williams Lake: Tarbell Facilitation Network, 2013.
7. "Text of Stephen Harper's Residential Schools Apology." CTV News. The Canadian Press. June 11, 2008. <https://www.ctvnews.ca/text-of-stephen-harper-s-residential-schools-apology-1.301820> accessed January, 2020.
8. "Indian Residential School apologies." Royal Canadian Mounted Police. November 29, 2019. <https://www.rcmp-grc.gc.ca/aboriginal-autochtone/apo-reg-eng.htm> Accessed April 20, 2020.
9. "Indian Residential School apologies." Royal Canadian Mounted Police. November 29, 2019. <https://www.rcmp-grc.gc.ca/aboriginal-autochtone/apo-reg-eng.htm> Accessed April 20, 2020. <"Truth and Reconciliation Commission - Expressions of Reconciliation." Royal Canadian Mounted Police, April 25, 2014. <https://www.youtube.com/watch?v=6JEEWYnUO4g> accessed April 30, 2020.
10. "The Role of the Royal Canadian Mounted Police During the Indian Residential School System." Government of Canada. Marcel-Eugéne LeBeuf. April 3, 2013. <http://publications.gc.ca/site/eng/9.651577/publication.html> accessed April 30, 2020. pp. 19.
11. "The Role of the Royal Canadian Mounted Police During the Indian Residential School System". Government of Canada. Marcel-Eugéne LeBeuf. April 3, 2013. <http://publications.gc.ca/site/eng/9.651577/publication.html> accessed April 30, 2020. pp. 1.
12 Tarbell, Harold. St. Joseph's Mission Residential School Commemoration Project Document. Remembering, Recovering, and Reconciling. Williams Lake: Tarbell Facilitation Network, 2013.
13. "Orange Shirt Society." Orange Shirt Day. <https://www.orangeshirtday.org/orange-shirt-society.html> accessed May 1, 2020.

A view of Saint Joseph's Mission Residential School in Williams Lake, BC. This is the Residential School that Phyllis Webstad attended. Photo by Dave Abott.

CHAPTER 2 SETTING THE STAGE
TO RESIDENTIAL SCHOOLS

In order to understand the importance of Orange Shirt Day, we must go back to the beginning and learn about the events that led to the creation of **Indian Residential Schools** in Canada. By understanding the mistakes made by past governments, and others throughout history, they can be prevented from happening in the future.

Orange Shirt Day is about ensuring that everyone understands the impacts of the Residential School System. Everyone must recognize that the Residential School System and events that occurred within the system were wrong, and that they feel empowered to help prevent these mistakes from ever happening again.

Before one can start talking about Residential Schools and their impacts, there are a few things you need to be aware of. Let's start at the very beginning, before Europeans and Indigenous people came into contact.

INDIGENOUS SOCIETY BEFORE CONTACT

For a long time, Indigenous people lived in what is now known as North America before Europeans arrived. All of these Indigenous cultures were unique yet they shared common worldviews. Indigenous communities had their own oral histories, common laws and ways of being.

"Historically Aboriginal people throughout North America lived in successful and dynamic societies. These societies have their own languages, history, cultures, spirituality, technologies, and values. The security and survival of these societies depended on passing on this legacy from one generation to the next. Aboriginal peoples did this through a seamless mixture of teachings, ceremonies, and daily activities. While differing in specifics from one people to another, traditional Aboriginal teachings described a coherent, interconnected world." [1]

Alicia Mae Cardinal performs a women's fancy orange shawl & dress dance special at a 2019 Pow Wow in Kamloops, B.C. Photo is by Peter Olsen of Olsen Imaging.

COLONIZATION IN CANADA

As Europeans began to explore and **colonize** this side of the world, Indigenous communities became threatened.[2] The government and the new settlers wanted to develop Indigenous land, but the Indigenous communities rightfully did not want to leave their traditional territories. As a result, the government and new settlers began mistreating the Indigenous people in a variety of cruel ways.

As European immigrants settled in Canada, they brought several diseases that gravely impacted the Indigenous people who did not have a natural immunity.[3] In 1862, a smallpox outbreak began in Victoria B.C., and then it spread to Indigenous communities throughout B.C. The outbreak of smallpox resulted in the deaths of approximately half of B.C.'s Indigenous population leaving their land vulnerable for colonization. [4]

Several years later, the Indian Act was created to continue the efforts to remove Indigenous people, their cultures and their traditions from Canada.

Artwork by grade 12 student Lauren Nichols.

Colonize occurs when settlers attempt to take over foreign land by forcefully imposing their own politics and culture.

THE INDIAN ACT

In 1876, the Canadian Government passed a law called the Indian Act under the leadership of John A. Macdonald, the first Prime Minister of Canada and Minister of Indian Affairs. The purpose of the Indian Act was to control, marginalize and oppress Indigenous people.[5]

The Indian Act gave the government political power enabling them to control the Indigenous population by regulating their languages, traditions, customs and lands. Indigenous people were required to register themselves and even live on government allotted land.

The Indian Act was maintained by the Department of Indian Affairs and Northern Development. Indian Agents were employed to ensure the Indigenous people were obeying the law; Indigenous people were completely stripped of their freedoms. The Indian Act is still in force today.

*"...the Indian Act... brought together all of Canada's legislation governing Indian people. The act both defined who Indians were under Canadian law and set out the process by which people would cease to be Indians. Under the act, the Canadian Government assumed control of Indian peoples' governments, economy, religion, land, education, and even their personal lives. The act empowered the federal cabinet to depose Chiefs and overturn **band** decisions—and the government used this authority to control band governments... Provisions in the Indian Act prohibited Indians from participating in sacred ceremonies such as the Potlatch on the West Coast and the Sun Dance on the Prairies. Indians could not own reserve land as individuals... The act placed new restrictions on Aboriginal hunting rights. The government had the power to move the bands if reserve land was needed by growing towns and cities."* [6]

Indian Act is a Canadian federal law enacted in 1876 that allowed the government the regimented management of Indigenous people and reserve lands. The purpose of the Indian Act was to control, marginalize and oppress Indigenous people. [7]

A Band "or 'Indian Band', is a governing unit of Indians in Canada instituted by the Indian Act, 1876. The Indian Act defines a 'band' as a 'body of Indians.'" [8]

LAND TAKEN

After the Indian Act was created, it shifted the life of Indigenous people in many negative ways including the loss of ability to practice cultural ceremonies, the loss of hunting rights and the implementation of government control over Indigenous communities.[9] The government wanted land and resources. Indigenous people were deemed to be in the way. Their land was taken and reserves were established often on useless infertile land, confining most Indigenous people to a specific area. [10]

INDIAN AGENTS

The **Indian Agent** was an administrator or representative for the Canadian government who had authority over Indigenous people and reserve lands.[11] As Phyllis Webstad explained "The Indian Agent had more power than the Chiefs and the Matriarchs." [12]

Artwork by Brock Nicol from Phyllis Webstad's children's book, *The Orange Shirt Story.*

ROYAL CANADIAN MOUNTED POLICE

The Royal Canadian Mounted Police played a role in the Indian Residential School System by responding to various law-enforcement related requests from Indian Agents and the Department of Indian Affairs. These requests included retrieving children who had run away from Residential School and fining families for not sending their children to Residential School. [13]

THE CREATION OF THE RESIDENTIAL SCHOOLS SYSTEM

When Indigenous children lived within their communities, prior to the creation of the Residential School System, Indigenous families had the ability to continue passing on cultural identity and customs to their children. In 1879, John A. MacDonald declared "it has been strongly impressed upon myself, as head of the [Indian] department, that Indian children should be withdrawn as much as possible from the parental influence, and the only way to do that would be to put them in central training industrial schools where they will acquire the habits and modes of thought of white men." [14]

John A Macdonald wanted to remove the children from their families to assimilate them into European-like culture. "[He] moved a measure through his cabinet authorizing the creation of three Residential Schools for Aboriginal children... What existed prior to 1883 was not a Residential School system, but a series of individual church-led initiatives... The federal government decision in that year to open three new schools on the prairies marked... the beginning of Canada's Residential School System." [15]

The first Residential School in Canada was called the Mohawk Institute; it is pictured here in 1943. The original school building was destroyed by fire in the 1850s and the replacement building was also destroyed by fire in 1903. The building pictured here served as the Mohawk Institute from 1904 to 1970 when it closed. Photo courtesy of the Shingwauk Residential Schools Centre of Algoma University.

John A Macdonald was the first prime minster of Canada. It was his government's decision to open three schools off reserve through government funding that marked "the beginning of Canada's Residential School System." [16]

In 1920, the Canadian Government changed the Indian Act *"to require school-aged Indian children to attend school."* [17] Indigenous children were now required to attend Residential School whether they wanted to or not. Initially there were three government sponsored Residential Schools in 1883. By 1931 there were eighty government sponsored Residential Schools across Canada. Duncan Campbell Scott, who succeeded John A Macdonald as Minister of Indian Affairs, announced, *"I want to get rid of the Indian problem… Our objective is to continue until there is not an Indian that has not been absorbed into the body politic, and there is no Indian question, and no Indian Department…"* [18]

Residential Schools were used as a way to remove Indigenous people, their cultures and their traditions from within Canada. The early to mid 1900s saw a dramatic rise in the quantity of Residential Schools, thus more and more children were separated from their families and communities.

…those of you who are interested in the Residential School story need to understand something that is very important, that it isn't just about Residential Schools. They [the Canadian Government] took our children away from us and placed them in the schools so that they could indoctrinate them into a different way of thinking… then they proceeded to go out and try to destroy the villages. So they undermined our leadership, they took away the power of Chiefs, they took away the power of women, they took away the power of our culture, they prohibited ceremonies, they prohibited gatherings, they prohibited all of the things that societies need to hold itself together. As many Survivors have observed, they took away our power. They took away our power to be who we were meant to be.

- Truth And Reconciliation Commission Chair Senator Murray Sinclair [19]

Senator Murray Sinclair speaking on reconciliation at King's University on September 26, 2019. Photo taken by Michael Swan of the Catholic Register.

The Canadian Government was intentional and systematic with their approach to settle the land and remove any trace of Indigenous peoples and their cultural practices.[20] Truth and Reconciliation Commission Chair Murray Sinclair described this as cultural **genocide** when delivering the report of the Commission.[21]

Understanding and learning the history of what happened before, during and after Residential Schools is critical to achieving reconciliation. Without knowing what happened and how it happened, change would be impossible. Through educating yourself on the creation of the Indian Act, the horrible things that followed and the establishment of government-sponsored Residential Schools, you can begin to become an agent of change.

A view outside St. Joseph's Mission Residential School (also known as Williams Lake Indian School). Year unknown. Photo courtesy of Fonds Deschâtelets, Archives Deschâtelets-NDC.

Genocide "means any of the following acts committed with intent to destroy, in whole or in part, a national, ethnical, racial or religious group, as such: Killing members of the group; Causing serious bodily or mental harm to members of the group; Deliberately inflicting on the group conditions of life calculated to bring about its physical destruction in whole or in part; Imposing measures intended to prevent births within the group; Forcibly transferring children of the group to another group." [22]

Every Child Matters

Artwork by grade 10 student Ava Scully showing a
child's appearance before and after Residential School.

CHAPTER TWO QUESTIONS

REVIEW

1. Before European contact with Indigenous people of North America, did Indigenous people have their own history, languages and cultures?

2. Based on the text, what impacts did European settlers have on Indigenous communities?

3. In 1862, which disease caused an outbreak in British Columbia? Why did so many Indigenous people die of this disease compared to Europeans?

4. What year did the Indian Act become law? How did the Indian Act affect Indigenous people?

5. Who was the leader of Canada when the Indian Act became law?

6. What is the reserve system in Canada?

7. What was the role of an Indian Agent?

8. What role did the RCMP play in the Residential School System?

9. In 1883, John A MacDonald made a decision that drastically impacted Indigenous children and their families. What was that decision?

10. In 1920, the Canadian Government changed the Indian Act for what purpose? How did this affect Indigenous children and families?

11. By 1931, how many government-sponsored Residential Schools existed in Canada?

12. Did genocide take place in Canada?

TIMELINE ACTIVITY

Complete the following timeline activity. Use the book and your own research if needed to create a timeline with the events of what took place.

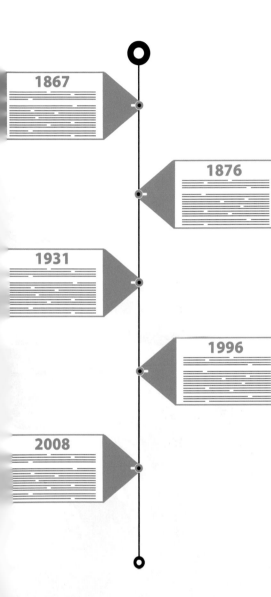

Dates:
1867, 2008, 1883, 1600s, 1876, 1996, 1931, 1920

Events:
First Non-Government-Sponsored Residential Schools Established

Date Canada Became a Country

Indian Act Becomes Law

Residential School System Becomes Government-Sponsored

Changes to Indian Act Making it Mandatory for Indigenous Children to Attend Residential Schools

By This Time There Were 80 Government-Sponsored Residential Schools

Last Government-Sponsored Residential School was Closed

The Canadian Government Issued an Apology to Indigenous People for their Role in Residential Schools

REFLECT

1. The Indian Act was designed to control, marginalize and oppress Indigenous people. What do you think the people who created the Indian Act thought about Indigenous people at that time?

2. In 1920, Indigenous children were forced into the Residential School System by the Canadian government making it mandatory for children to attend Residential Schools. How do you think this impacted Indigenous children and communities?

3. The Orange Shirt Society believes reconciliation requires each of us to have a thorough understanding of Canadian and Indigenous history before, during and after the Indian Residential School System. Why do you think it is important to understand and talk about this history in order to achieve reconciliation?

RESEARCH

1. Look up the Indian Act. How does the Indian Act continue to affect Indigenous peoples today?

2. What are the traditional systems of governance in Indigenous communities? How do they operate? What is the role of the Chief or Matriarch in some communities? Please note there is a variety and diversity of cultures and therefore the same can be found in traditional governing systems. In your research, ensure you honour specific cultures and peoples.

3. In the final page of the chapter, the term Genocide is used. What other countries have experienced a genocide?

SOURCES

1. The Truth and Reconciliation Commission of Canada. They Came for the Children. Manitoba: Library and Archives Canada Cataloguing in Publication, 2012. pp. 7.
2. "Indigenous History in Canada." Indigenous and Northern Affairs Canada. August 14, 2018. <https://www.aadnc-aandc.gc.ca/eng/1100100013778/1100100013779> accessed February 1, 2020.
3. "The Impacts of Smallpox on First Nations on the West Coast." Indigenous Corporate Training. April 17, 2017. <https://www.ictinc.ca/blog/the-impact-of-smallpox-on-first-nations-on-the-west-coast> accessed May 1, 2020.
4. "Smallpox in Canada." The Canadian Encyclopedia. February 12, 2020. <https://www.thecanadianencyclopedia.ca/en/article/smallpox> accessed May 28, 2020.
5. The Truth and Reconciliation Commission of Canada. They Came for the Children. Manitoba: Library and Archives Canada Cataloguing in Publication, 2012. pp. 18.
6. The Truth and Reconciliation Commission of Canada. They Came for the Children. Manitoba: Library and Archives Canada Cataloguing in Publication, 2012. pp. 11.
7. The Truth and Reconciliation Commission of Canada. They Came for the Children. Manitoba: Library and Archives Canada Cataloguing in Publication, 2012. pp. 11.
8. "Bands." Indigenous Foundations UBC Arts. <https://indigenousfoundations.arts.ubc.ca/bands/>, accessed May 25, 2020.
9. "Reserves." The Canadian Encyclopedia, July 12, 2018. < https://www.thecanadianencyclopedia.ca/en/article/aboriginal-reserves> accessed May 28, 2020.
10. "Canada's Residential Schools: The History, Part 1 Origins to 1939." Truth and Reconciliation Commission of Canada. 2015. <http://www.trc.ca/assets/pdf/Volume_1_History_Part_1_English_Web.pdf> accessed May 30, 2020. pp. 3.
11. "Indian Agents in Canada." The Canadian Encyclopedia, October 25, 2018. < https://www.thecanadianencyclopedia.ca/en/article/indian-agents-in-canada> accessed May 28, 2020.
12. Webstad, Phyllis. Personal Interview. January. 2020.
13. "The Role of the Royal Canadian Mounted Police During the Indian Residential School System. "Government of Canada. Marcel-Eugéne LeBeuf. April 3, 2013. <http://publications.gc.ca/site/eng/9.651577/publication.html> accessed April 30, 2020.
14. "10 Quotes John A. Macdonald Made About First Nations." Indigenous Corporate Training. June 28, 2016. < https://www.ictinc.ca/blog/10-quotes-john-a.-macdonald-made-about-first-nations> accessed May 28, 2020.
15. The Truth and Reconciliation Commission of Canada. They Came for the Children. Manitoba: Library and Archives Canada Cataloguing in Publication, 2012. pp. 5-6.
16. The Truth and Reconciliation Commission of Canada. They Came for the Children. Manitoba: Library and Archives Canada Cataloguing in Publication, 2012. pp. 6.
17. The Truth and Reconciliation Commission of Canada. They Came for the Children. Manitoba: Library and Archives Canada Cataloguing in Publication, 2012. pp. 12.

"Indian Residential Schools and Reconciliation: 1920-1927 Indian Act Becomes More Restrictive." First Nations Education Steering Committee. <http://www.fnesc.ca/wp/wp-content/uploads/2015/07/IRSR11-12-DE-1920-1927.pdf> accessed May 28, 2020.

18. "10 Quotes John A. Macdonald Made About First Nations." Indigenous Corporate Training. June 28, 2016. < https://www.ictinc.ca/blog/10-quotes-john-a.-macdonald-made-about-first-nations> accessed May 28, 2020.
19. "Justice and Federal Commissioner Murray Sinclair Speech." Truth and Reconciliation Commission. The Commemoration Project Events. Filmed by John Dell. Signal Point Media, 2013. DVD.
20. "Canada's Residential Schools: The History, Part 1 Origins to 1939." Truth and Reconciliation Commission of Canada. 2015. <http://www.trc.ca/assets/pdf/Volume_1_History_Part_1_English_Web.pdf> accessed May 30, 2020. pp. 4.
21. "Residential Schools Finding Point to 'Cultural Genocide,' Commission Chair Say." CBC News. John Paul Tasker. May 30, 2015. <https://www.cbc.ca/news/politics/residential-schools-findings-point-to-cultural-genocide-commission-chair-says-1.3093580> accessed January 15, 2020.
22. "Genocide" United Nations Office on Genocide Prevention and the Responsibility to Protect. <https://www.un.org/en/genocideprevention/genocide.shtml> accessed February 15, 2020.

CHAPTER

3 RESIDENTIAL SCHOOLS
THE EFFECTS ON INDIGENOUS PEOPLE

In order to begin the process of reconciliation it is crucial for all people to learn what took place in Residential Schools.

It is estimated that approximately 150,000 Indigenous children attended government-sponsored Canadian Residential Schools.[1] At least 6000 of those children died at Residential Schools due to a variety of reasons including abuse, overcrowding, malnourishment, neglect, poor health and trying to run away.[2] These government Residential Schools ran between 1883 and 1996. As of 2015, it was estimated that there were over 80,000 Survivors of Residential Schools. [3]

Chief Fred Robbins' vision of reconciling requires all people to understand the truths of what happened in Residential Schools and for this history to be taught in schools. When everyone understands and acknowledges the truths of the impact of Residential Schools, reconciling our differences and finding a path forward for a better future becomes possible.

It is important to remember each Residential School Survivor may have had a different experience but there are common stories amongst all Survivors.

THE LOCATION OF RESIDENTIAL SCHOOLS

Many Residential Schools were in isolated locations across Canada. This was a deliberate strategy of the government to remove children from their parental and cultural influences.

"When the school is on the reserve, the child lives with his parents who are savages; he is surrounded by savages, and though he may learn to read and write, his habits and training and mode of thought are Indian."

-John A Macdonald [4]

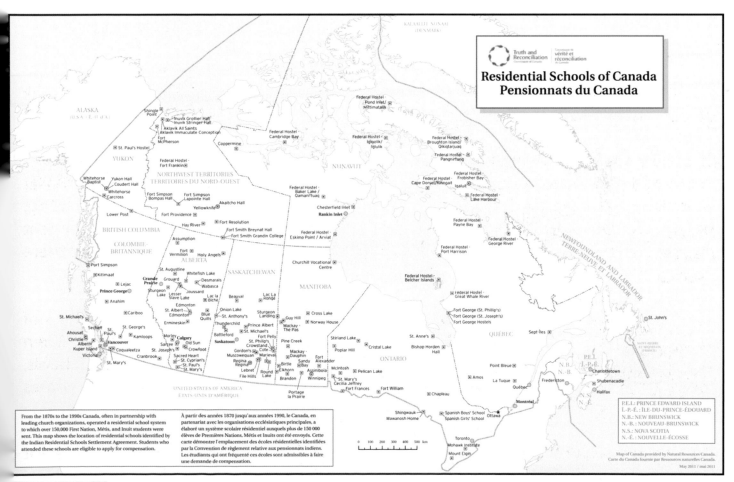

Truth and Reconciliation Commission map showing only government funded Residential Schools in Canada.

In 1920, the Indian Act was amended to require all Indigenous children to attend Residential School.[5] Indigenous families had no choice, and the Canadian government forced children to leave their parents and families behind to attend Residential School when they were as young as four years old. Children were isolated and deprived of their families, culture, language, communities and security.

Phyllis Webstad and her aunt, Agness Jack, at the first Orange Shirt Day event in Williams Lake in 2013. Photo taken by Monica Lamb-Yorski of the Williams Lake Tribune.

I was six years old, and I'll never forget seeing that place for the first time. We came through the Onward Ranch and I got this terrible feeling - you know, like you have to not feel emotions any more? Like they're pushed down - and I just knew I was going to prison.

- Residential School Survivor Agness Jack, Aunt of Phyllis Webstad [6]

Young boy named Thomas Moore is pictured before and after he was admitted to the Regina Indian Industrial School in May of 1874. This photo is courtesy of Library and Archives Canada and the Annual Report of the Department of Indian Affairs, 1896/OCLC 1771148.

THE ARRIVAL AT RESIDENTIAL SCHOOLS

The arrival at Residential School was traumatic and difficult for many children.

"The assault on Aboriginal Identity began the moment the child took the first step across the school's threshold… Braided hair, which often has spiritual significance, was cut." [7]

When children arrived at Residential School their hair was cut and they were stripped of their clothes. Residential School Survivors have noted harsh chemicals were used to clean children upon arrival. In some cases, children were given a number and referred to by that number instead of their name. Some Survivors reported being given a new name entirely.

Cutting children's hair and taking away their names and clothes were the first steps in stripping children of their identity and self-worth.

LIFE AT RESIDENTIAL SCHOOLS

Life at the Residential Schools was traumatic and regimented. Days were filled with chores and religious teachings. Many children experienced unimaginable emotional, physical and sexual abuse creating trauma for which they were never given the opportunity or resources to heal. The Residential School housed children for the majority of the year and offered minimal, if any, education.[8] At Residential Schools, students were required to learn skills such as housekeeping and trades. Ultimately, their new skills served to keep the schools in operation as well as provided free labour for the school-run businesses. [9]

Students were swiftly and harshly punished for speaking their Indigenous languages. Due to funding issues, overcrowding and neglect "the schools could neither teach or care for children." [10]

A view inside St. Joseph's Mission Residential School (also know as Williams Lake Indian School) bedroom quarters with the students performing their prayers. Year unknown. Photo courtesy of Fonds Deschâtelets, Archives Deschâtelets-NDC.

A view inside the chapel at St. Joseph's Mission Residential School (also know as Williams Lake Indian School). Year unknown. Photo courtesy of Fonds Deschâtelets, Archives Deschâtelets-NDC.

RELIGIOUS INFLUENCE AT RESIDENTIAL SCHOOLS

Residential Schools in Canada were maintained and run by many religious groups including the Anglican, Baptist, Catholic, Mennonite, Non-denominational, Presbyterian and United Churches. The Canadian Government and churches not only wanted Indigenous people to adopt new western and colonial values, but they also wanted them to become more Christian. Residential Schools were staffed by members of these religious groups and churches who forced the students to suppress their own beliefs and adopt Christian values resulting in spiritual abuse. Their goal was to "civilize and Christianize" the students.[11] Many of these religious leaders took advantage of the students through emotional, physical and sexual abuses causing life long trauma that was later transmitted to other family members and generations.

"Churches were eager to embrace the partnership [with government] because church missionary societies had laid the foundation for the system. For most of the system's history, the churches had responsibility for the day-to-day operation of the schools... [the church] provided justification for undermining traditional spiritual leaders (who were treated as agents of the devil), banning sacred cultural practices, and attempting to impose a new moral code on Aboriginal people by requiring them to abandon their traditional family structures." [12]

ST. JOSEPH'S MISSION RESIDENTIAL SCHOOL

St. Joseph's Mission Residential School, or 'The Mission,' was the Residential School that both Phyllis Webstad and Chief Fred Robbins attended, among many other Survivors from the Cariboo region.

"The St. Joseph's Mission Residential School... was founded and operated by the Oblates of Mary Immaculate, a French order of the Roman Catholic Church whose missionaries had been associated with the Cariboo region since the early days of contact and fur trading. The St. Joseph's Mission was [originally one] of the earliest churches in the valley and is approximately 10km south of the City of Williams Lake. The school opened in 1872 and originally served as a day school for the children of miners.

In 1891, the Oblate Fathers and the Federal Government agreed to operate the school exclusively as an industrial Residential School for native children... The 'official dates' for the operation of the school are July 19, 1891 to June 30,1981. The school buildings were eventually torn down and the property sold. Today, the foundation is all that remains of the school, along with the cemetery and the remainder of the property operates as a ranch." [13]

Historical photo of Saint Joseph's Mission Residential School. Photo courtesy of John Dell.

St. Joseph's Mission Residential School was located just outside of Williams Lake, B.C. It opened in 1872 and closed in 1981. St. Joseph's Mission Residential School has also been called The Mission, Williams Lake Indian School, Williams Lake Industrial School, Cariboo Residential Industrial School and Cariboo Student Residence.

The school was supported by an annual federal grant, but funding was a constant issue and often inadequate to support quality education, care of children, or facility maintenance. The school was attended by children from the three nearby Nations, [the Secwépemc (Shuswap), the Tsilhqot'in (Chilcotin) and the Dakelh (Carrier)] as well as from the St'at'imc (Lillooet) Nation...

Teaching methods at The Mission required unquestioning obedience, strict discipline and speaking only in English. Transgressions resulted in harsh punishment. Hunger was common, food often poor, and sickness rampant in the poorly constructed buildings. The school attempted to destroy students' pride in their heritage, their families and themselves... The student death rate was high, and some who died were not returned to their parents.

- Written by Ordell Steen, Jean William and Rick Gilbert in the *Orange Shirt Story*. [14]

Agness Jack photographed by Darrin Andrews

Former St. Joseph's Mission Residential School student Agness Jack reflects on her horrific experience and the effects it had on her.

"

During that first year [at the Residential School], I contracted tuberculosis. I was sick for a long time, and they treated me very badly. I was very sick, and finally I was sent to Coqualeetza Indian Hospital in Sardis. It was a Residential School but they turned it into a sanitarium for Indian people with TB because there were so many of us. I was there four years, and it was a blessing in disguise because they treated us like people - you know, like you should get treated in a hospital when you are sick, and the food was way better. It sure was a shock to me when I went back to the Mission - they called us by numbers instead of names, we were treated as kids without feelings.

Once at Easter, after I got out, my mom wanted me to go to Mass on Easter Sunday. I told her that I went to church enough at the Mission to last me the rest of my life, and what good did it do me? That Bishop... preached the best sermons - he was the head of the school, the principal - and look what he did! He travelled with the girls in the pipe band, and he molested them - he drove the bus. He was tried in Vancouver but his case was dismissed or postponed on a technicality. I think the women just didn't have it in them to go through all that again. So he never paid for what he did.

I was working as a reporter for the Tribune when the place finally closed, and I went to cover the final Mass for the paper. I overheard the night watchman talking with another man, and he said, 'It's about time that place closed'. Those children were supposed to be brought here for education, and instead they were sent to hell. [15]

"

INTERGENERATIONAL TRAUMA

The trauma created by Residential Schools has created long-term impacts that have affected family members who did not attend a Residential School themselves. Many of the former students were unable to care for themselves or their families which created trauma passed down through the generations. Intergenerational trauma is still felt today within Indigenous communities.

Many of us have not attended Residential School including myself but we feel the impacts, our children feel it, our grandchildren feel it. Today and yesterday is the beginning of a very small step in reconciliation between all communities and the Residential Schools that have impacted our First Nations people. I spoke yesterday about the high numbers of incarceration and low education levels of our First Nations People. The high number of children that are in care. Those are direct results and impacts from the Residential School. We need to start someway to find a way to break that cycle and start having our people become healthier. It's an interesting and a long journey.

- Former Chief Ann Louie of Williams Lake Indian Band (T'exelcemc) [16]

Former Chief Ann Louie speaking at the May 17, 2013 unveiling of a commemorative monument in Boitanio Park, Williams Lake, BC. Film still courtesy of John Dell.

LIFE AFTER RESIDENTIAL SCHOOLS

Life after Residential Schools has been extremely difficult and painful for many Indigenous people across Canada. The trauma and pain of Residential Schools has affected Survivors and their families creating intergenerational trauma.

Intergenerational trauma occurs when the trauma experienced by a parent or grandparent is also experienced by future generations, both emotionally and physically. The results of the intergenerational trauma caused by Residential Schools are catastrophic and have taken form in many ways such as alcoholism, abuse, mental illness and children being forced to live in foster care.[17]

As the government succeeded at suppressing traditional Indigenous skills and customs and separating children from their parents, the children were left parentless and unable to pass down traditional knowledge to their own families creating a significant loss of culture.

Intergenerational Survivors are Indigenous people who are still affected by the experiences of their ancestors who attended Residential Schools. The trauma has been transmitted from one family member to another due to the fact that the trauma runs so deep and that the Indigenous peoples were not provided with the resources to heal from their painful experiences.[18]

Orange Shirt Day acknowledges this intergenerational trauma and the pain experienced by Survivors and their families. Through this movement everyone is able to witness and share the collective truths of the trauma endured by not only Residential School Survivors, but their families thereafter.

In order to heal the wounds of the Residential School System, we must create a new legacy that "Every Child Matters." Through the acknowledgment of the painful truths of Residential Schools, and the cultural genocide that took place in Canada, we are able to begin healing and reconciling the trauma still felt today.

Intergenerational trauma is the transmission of historical oppression and its negative consequences across generations. [19]

Intergenerational survivor "refers to an individual who has been affected by the intergenerational dysfunction created by the experience of attending Residential School." [20]

Nanenuŵes?in (I will see you again)

"This image is in honour of my late Uncle Kelsey who passed away years after attending Residential School. My uncle is shown as an adult carrying his childhood spirit on his shoulders. As an adult, my uncle was a tough, loud guy and he wouldn't put up with mistreatment of himself, his loved ones and his nieces and nephews. So much is unsaid about some of the complications and challenges he experienced in his lifetime due to Residential School but we knew he dealt with a lot. I see my uncle every time I meet a tough-as-nails youth. A young person who has had to build up a thick exterior based on the accumulation of experiences and hardships they've faced and I honour these youth because they deserve our love, patience, and trust. My uncle deserved this, too."

by Karlene Harvey [21]

RESILIENCE

The Residential School System set out to assimilate Indigenous people into mainstream society. Indigenous children were treated poorly, removed from their families and taught to feel worthless. Although these experiences created a lot of trauma in the Indigenous community, the Residential School system did not accomplish its goal. Indigenous languages, cultures, ceremonies and families are being revitalized because of the **resilience** of the people. [22]

Keisha Jones dancing at the 2019 Orange Shirt Day in Victoria, B.C. Photo taken by Eden Sunflower.

Keisha Jones dancing at the 2019 Orange Shirt Day in Victoria, B.C.:
"*My families Yakima lineage is where our connection to the powwow circle stems. It is through these lines that I have learned to dance. The style I practice is fancy shawl and represents the butterfly. I choose to dance in settings such as Orange Shirt Day to honour the lives lost a Residential Schools and the resilience in our communities. I dance to inspire the young ones, show them how dancing can empower them in their identities and help heal their wounds. I dance to honour the spirits of those who have walked before us and those who have passed on. I dance to lift the spirits of the Elders present and those who can no longer dance.*" [23]

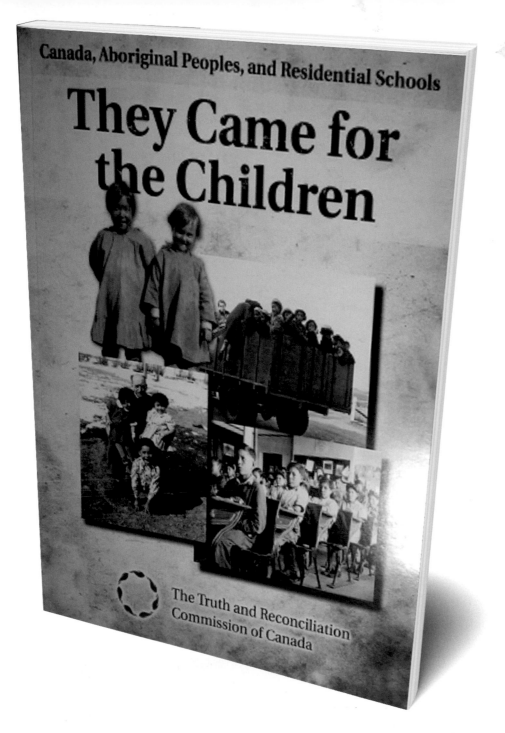

Canada, Aboriginal Peoples, and Residential Schools

They Came for the Children

The Truth and Reconciliation
Commission of Canada

TRUTH AND RECONCILIATION COMMISSION RESOURCES

The Truth and Reconciliation Commission of Canada (TRC) has created resources that can be used to effectively understand the truth of what took place in the Residential School System. Some resources included *They Came for the Children* (interim report), the TRC final report which gives 94 calls to action for change and a map of government-sponsored Residential Schools in Canada. The map can be found at the front of this book. These are all excellent resources to further understand what took place in the Residential School System.

CHAPTER THREE QUESTIONS

REVIEW

1. How many children are recorded as attending government-sponsored Residential Schools in Canada?

2. Even though the records are incomplete, how many children are presumed to have not returned home from Residential School?

3. During which years did government-sponsored Residential Schools run?

4. As of 2020, how many Residential School Survivors are alive?

5. Why were many Residential Schools located in isolated areas?

6. What happened to children when they arrived at Residential Schools? What happened to their clothes, and why? How were the students treated?

7. What was life like for children at Residential Schools?

8. What role did churches play in the Residential School System?

9. When did St. Joseph's Mission Indian Residential School open? When did it close? Where was it located?

10. What is intergenerational trauma? Are there intergenerational Survivors alive today?

ACTIVITY

Express yourself - The feeling of arriving at Residential School.

How would you feel being separated from your families and loved ones as young as six-years-old? Paint, draw and/or write what comes to your mind.

REFLECT

1. What do you think it was like for children, some as young as two, four and six-years-old, who were forced to leave their families and attend Residential Schools for the first time? How do you think those children felt being forced to leave their families and communities?

2. Why do you think we refer to Residential School Survivors and Intergenerational Survivors as "Survivors" instead of victims. How could the choice of words affect their journey?

3. What is resilience? How does a cultural resurgence relate to resilience?

4. What do you think the purpose was behind students being given numbers in place of their names while attending Residential Schools?

RESEARCH

1. Do you know if there was a Residential School in your area? Can you name the school?

2. Find a book that details the personal accounts of Indigenous people who attended Residential Schools. Ask your librarian or a teacher for help or visit our website for more resources at www.medicinewheel.education/orangeshirtday

3. Look up St. Joseph's Mission Indian Residential School definition. Take note of the different names of the Residential School. One of those names is Williams Lake Industrial School. Research why the word 'Industrial' was used in reference to Residential School.

4. Did some children run away from Residential Schools? Hint: research Chanie Wenjack.

5. When Indigenous Residential School students spoke in their traditional languages or practiced their cultural customs, what happened to them?

6. Was Canada the only country to have Residential Schools?

SOURCES

1. "Truth and Reconciliation Commissions: By the Numbers." CBC News. Daniel Schwartz. June 2, 2015. <https://www.cbc.ca/news/indigenous/truth-and-reconciliation-commission-by-the-numbers-1.3096185> accessed May 28, 2020.
2. "Truth and Reconciliation Commissions: By the Numbers." CBC News. Daniel Schwartz. June 2, 2015. <https://www.cbc.ca/news/indigenous/truth-and-reconciliation-commission-by-the-numbers-1.3096185> accessed May 28, 2020.
3. "Truth and Reconciliation Commissions: By the Numbers." CBC News. Daniel Schwartz. June 2, 2015. <https://www.cbc.ca/news/indigenous/truth-and-reconciliation-commission-by-the-numbers-1.3096185> accessed May 28, 2020.
4. "10 Quotes John A. Macdonald Made About First Nations." Indigenous Corporate Training. June 28, 2016. < https://www.ictinc.ca/blog/10-quotes-john-a.-macdonald-made-about-first-nations > accessed May 28, 2020.
5. "Indian Residential Schools and Reconciliation: 1920-1927 Indian Act Becomes More Restrictive." First Nations Education Steering Committee. <http://www.fnesc.ca/wp/wp-content/uploads/2015/07/IRSR11-12-DE-1920-1927.pdf> accessed May 28, 2020.
6. Webstad, Phyllis. Joan Sorley, Tiffany Moses and Harold Tarbell. St. Joseph's Mission Residential School Commemoration Project Booklet. Remembering, Recovering, and Reconciling. Williams Lake: Tarbell Facilitation Network, 2013. pp. 6.
7. The Truth and Reconciliation Commission of Canada. They Came for the Children. Manitoba: Library and Archives Canada Cataloguing in Publication, 2012. pp. 22.
8. The Truth and Reconciliation Commission of Canada. They Came for the Children. Manitoba: Library and Archives Canada Cataloguing in Publication, 2012. pp. 30, 34, 41, 44.

    "Residential Schools in Canada." The Canadian Encyclopedia. January 15, 2020. < https://www.thecanadianencyclopedia.ca/en/article/residential-schools#LifeatResidentialSchools> accessed June 1, 2020.
9. "Canada's Residential Schools: The History, Part 1 Origins to 1939." Truth and Reconciliation Commission of Canada. 2015. <http://www.trc.ca/assets/pdf/Volume_1_History_Part_1_English_Web.pdf> accessed May 30, 2020. pp. 337.
10. The Truth and Reconciliation Commission of Canada. They Came for the Children. Manitoba: Library and Archives Canada Cataloguing in Publication, 2012. pp. 18.
11. The Truth and Reconciliation Commission of Canada. They Came for the Children. Manitoba: Library and Archives Canada Cataloguing in Publication, 2012. pp. 10.
12. The Truth and Reconciliation Commission of Canada. They Came for the Children. Manitoba: Library and Archives Canada Cataloguing in Publication, 2012. pp. 13.
13. Webstad, Phyllis. Joan Sorley, Tiffany Moses and Harold Tarbell. St. Joseph's Mission Residential School Commemoration Project Booklet. Remembering, Recovering, and Reconciling. Williams Lake: Tarbell Facilitation Network, 2013. pp. 4-5.
14. Webstad, Phyllis. The Orange Shirt Story. Medicine Wheel Education, Victoria. Printed: PRC. September 1, 2018.
15. Webstad, Phyllis. Joan Sorley, Tiffany Moses and Harold Tarbell. St. Joseph's Mission Residential School Commemoration Project Booklet. Remembering, Recovering, and Reconciling. Williams Lake: Tarbell Facilitation Network, 2013. pp. 6.
16. "Chief Ann Louie Speech." Boitanio Park Monument Unveiling. The Commemoration Project Events. Filmed by John Dell. Signal Point Media, 2013. DVD.
17. "The Intergenerational Trauma of First Nations Still Run Deep." The Global and Mail. Kevin Berube. February 16, 2015. <https://www.theglobeandmail.com/life/health-and-fitness/health-advisor/the-intergenerational-trauma-of-first-nations-still-runs-deep/article23013789/> accessed May 24, 2020.
18. "The Intergenerational Trauma of First Nations Still Run Deep." The Global and Mail. Kevin Berube. February 16, 2015. <https://www.theglobeandmail.com/life/health-and-fitness/health-advisor/the-intergenerational-trauma-of-first-nations-still-runs-deep/article23013789/> accessed May 24, 2020.
19. "Intervention to address Intergenerational Trauma." <https://www.ucalgary.ca/wethurston/files/wethurston/Report_InterventionToAddressIntergenerationalTrauma.pdf> accessed May 1, 2020.
20. "Intergenerational Survivors." Where are the Children. November 28, 2013. <http://wherearethechildren.ca/en/watc_blackboard/intergenerational-survivors/> accessed May 10, 2020.
21. Harvey, Karlene. Personal Interview. April. 2020.
22. Webstad, Phyllis. Personal Interview. January. 2020.
23. Jones, Keisha. Personal Interview. May. 2020.

CHAPTER 4 REMEMBERING
RECOVERING AND RECONCILING

Orange Shirt Day is a legacy of the St. Joseph's Mission Residential School Commemoration Project that took place in Williams Lake, B.C., Canada, in May 2013. The vision of Chief Fred Robbins of Esk'etemc (Alkali Lake), who is a former Residential School student himself, inspired a series of events that would lead to the creation of Orange Shirt Day. These events brought together Indigenous and non-Indigenous people with one vision and one common goal, reconciliation.

These events were designed to witness Residential School Survivor's truths, to honour their healing journey and that of their families, and to commit to the ongoing process of reconciliation. Former Chief Justice Murray Sinclair challenged all of the participants to keep the reconciliation process alive, as a result of the realization that every former student had similar stories.

"It was important for all people to know that everyone was welcome and invited to attend events. This was a project for all people to honour Survivors and listen to their stories. We wanted and needed to include everyone for reconciliation to happen."

- Phyllis Webstad[1]

It was at one of these events that Phyllis Webstad was encouraged to share her story as a Residential School Survivor, sowing the seeds for the creation of Orange Shirt Day.

...eyview Secondary School student Isacc Baptiste draws Orange Shirt Day inspired artwork for his Secwépemctsin class in 2019.

CHIEF FRED ROBBINS' VISION

Chief Fred Robbins' vision for reconciliation began when he realized that non-Indigenous residents of Williams Lake and the Cariboo area were completely unaware that St. Joseph's Mission Residential School was operating until recently in their midst. He knew that in order to create positive change for the future the entire community needed to hear the truths of what happened, and create a safe space in which the Survivors and their families could begin the process of healing. Chief Fred stated, *"We're ready to move forward and build relationships; to build a new legacy for the First Nations people, not one built on mistrust ..."* [2]

I first started this plan about five or six years ago [pre-2013]... and when I got the First Nations end of it done I realized that we know what happened, but the people of Williams Lake, Quesnel, 100 Miles, Wells, Lilloet don't... I need you as non-First Nations to make this a reality by coming and participating. This is the very first reconciliation project in the country that involved non-First Nations people.

- Chief Fred Robbins [3]

Chief Fred's vision was to put an epitaph in the form of a monument to remember those children who did not survive Residential School including those who died later as a result of their traumatic experiences. He knew he could not do it alone and reached out to the community for support. Community members rallied around Chief Fred's vision of the reconciliation monuments which blossomed into the St. Joseph's Mission Residential School Commemoration Project.

ST. JOSEPH'S MISSION RESIDENTIAL SCHOOL COMMEMORATION PROJECT

Chief Fred's vision soon started a passionate project that aimed to bring reconciliation to the Cariboo region. The project included a series of significant events in April and May 2013 that acknowledged Residential Schools and discussed the process of reconciliation, ultimately starting the healing and recovering journey for many.[4] To make this project happen, a committee formed to plan the events.

THE PROJECT PLANNING COMMITTEE

People in the Cariboo region understood and supported Chief Fred's vision of reconciliation and a planning committee was born to make his vision a reality. The planning committee was comprised of a diverse group of people who were supported by other locals and organizations. Together they organized a series of events that would pave a new path forward.

During the planning a theme emerged — remembering, recovering and reconciling. It acknowledged the need for truth telling and healing to happen before reconciliation could be achieved.

The Project Planning Committee from left to right: Chief Fred Robbins, Jerome Beauchamp (School District 27), Anne Burrill (City of Williams Lake), Eric Chrona (Royal Canadian Mounted Police), Joan Sorley (Cariboo Regional District), Rick Gilbert (Williams Lake Indian Band), David DeRose (School District 27), late Phillip Robbins, and Phyllis Webstad (St. Joseph Mission Residential School Survivor), Tiffany Moses (Mentored youth), Harold Tarbell (Tarbell Facilitation Network)

ST. JOSEPH'S MISSION COMMEMORATION PROJECT EVENTS [5]

April 23, 2013 - Planning Committee Press Conference at Thompson Rivers University

April 26, 2013 - SD 27 professional Development Day at Williams Lake Secondary School

April 28, 2013 - Public showing of youth and student mentored videos at Williams Lake Secondary School

May 13-19, 2013 - Private Truth and Reconciliation Commission individual statement gathering at Thompson Rivers University

May 16-17, 2013 - Commemoration Conference and Town Hall on Reconciliation with the TRC at Thompson Rivers University

May 16, 2013 - Monument unveiling ceremony at former St. Joseph's Mission Site

May 17, 2013 - Monument unveiling ceremony at Boitanio Park

May 18, 2013 - TRC public testimony gathering at Thompson Rivers University

May 18-19, 2013 - Former Residential School Student's Reunion at Williams Lake First Nation Pow Wow Arbor

At the time of the commemoration project events in 2013, Kerry Cook was the Mayor of Williams Lake. Chief Fred consulted with Kerry to get the city of Williams Lake involved in the process of reconciliation. Kerry was inspired by Chief Fred, his vision and his passion to create change. She didn't hesitate to become involved and the experience created an awakening within.

I still remember the day when Chief Fred Robbins walked into my Mayor's office. It changed my life, although I didn't know at the time how significant that really was.

As he started to share his story of reconciliation and his vision from his heart, I could feel his passion, his pain and his hope for what could be our future. It was powerful. I remember his courage for speaking his truth. His strength and vulnerability came from somewhere deep inside of him and as he shared his story it stirred or awakened something deep inside me.

It is not very often that you experience a divine encounter; a shared vision that awakens your very soul. Looking back it was as though the soil of my heart had been prepared for this very moment. When he shared his vision it was as though he was planting a seed deep into my heart. As we walked out the journey of reconciliation together I saw him grow stronger and stronger. Every tear was not wasted or forgotten, they watered that seed and it grew larger than I could ever imagine.

The actual truth and reconciliation event far exceeded any of my (our) expectations. Something powerful happened - the atmosphere shifted and Orange Shirt Day was birthed. That same courage; the inner strength to be real and vulnerable was also inside of Phyllis.

We all have a story - and as we share our stories we free others to share their stories as well. That is when it is possible to be agents of change, agents of possibilities and true agents of reconciliation.

- Former Mayor Kerry Cook, of Williams Lake, B.C. [6]

Chief Fred Robbins, former Mayor Kerry Cook and Debra Robbins at the first Orange Shirt Day in Williams Lake in 2013. Photo is courtesy of the City of Williams Lake.

THE MOMENT THE SEED FOR ORANGE SHIRT DAY WAS PLANTED

As part of the commemorative events a Residential School Survivor's reunion was being planned by a committee. That committee asked Phyllis Webstad to represent their group at the April 23, 2013, press conference to kick off the week of events. Phyllis was nervous about speaking and didn't know what she was going to say. Phyllis asked her friend, Joan Sorley, who was also working on the St. Joseph's Mission Commemoration Project, to meet for coffee and discuss her upcoming speech.

Residential School Survivor Phyllis Webstad, School District #27 Superintendent Mark Thiessen, Chair of the Cariboo CRD Al Richmond, Former Williams Lake Mayor Kerry Cook and Chief Fred Robbins at the press conference promoting St. Joseph's Mission Commemoration Project in 2013 at Boitanio Park in Williams Lake. Photo taken by Monica Lamb-Yorski of the Williams Lake Tribune.

"*I met Joan at the Bean Counter, a local coffee shop. Joan and I were to meet and discuss what I would say at the press conference the next morning, I was very nervous. Joan could only meet later in the day, so at like 4:15 or so we decided to meet. Joan was already there. I stood in line for my coffee and by the time I was sitting down I knew what I would talk about the next day. I get choked up everytime I tell this part. I sat down and told Joan I knew what I was going to talk about, my first day at Residential School. I immediately had tears streaming down my face and told Joan the story. When I finished, I realized I had nothing orange in my closet and that I needed to get shopping. By this time it was close to five and stores in Williams Lake close by six so I didn't have much time. I went to my favorite women's clothing store. I couldn't find an orange shirt but I did find an orange mesh sweater, so I bought that and that's what I wore. In the photo of us in the park you can see all the people with titles, Chief, Superintendent, Mayor, CRD Chair then there's me, unemployed Residential School Survivor... in bright orange!*"

- Phyllis Webstad[7]

In Williams Lake in 2013, Phyllis Webstad shared her story about her orange shirt publicly for the first time. Photo taken by Monica Lamb-Yorski of the Williams Lake Tribune.

At the press conference, for the first time, Phyllis Webstad publicly spoke about her story of her orange shirt and her experience attending Residential School. This is what Phyllis had to say:

> *My name is Phyllis Webstad... I went to St. Joseph's when I had just turned six in 1973-1974. I just went for one year... I'm the third generation. My grandmother went for ten years... my mother went and I went... My grandmother probably couldn't afford it but she always bought a new set of clothes for all the kids going to the Mission and I was no exception. It was really exciting. I picked out an orange shirt and it was really shiny and it just sparkled... When I got there we got stripped... my orange shirt was taken away... To me orange has never been my friend. So I wear it today as a symbol of the healing that is taking place. Orange has always been to me... not mattering to anyone, nobody cared that we had feelings... just being insignificant. So to me that's what orange means. Today, that's why I wear it. That's not the case anymore.*

- Phyllis Webstad[8]

ST. JOSEPH'S MISSION COMMEMORATIVE MONUMENTS

There were many events that took place during the week-long commemoration project. The Orange Shirt Society would like to highlight the ceremonies where two commemorative 'brother and sister' monuments were raised. *"Two monuments are dedicated: one at the site of St. Joseph's Mission School to memorialize the former students and the other in Boitanio park in Williams Lake to jointly commit to shared reconciliation. Both monuments contain excerpts from Prime Minister Stephen Harper's and the Oblates of Mary Immaculate's official apologies."*[9] Communities from near and far came to both ceremonies to honour the former students and their families.

So here we are, the city of Williams Lake, the First Nations in and around. The 15 bands. We stand here in front of, hopefully, a new legacy. Creating a future for our children. 'Every Child Matters,' as the National Chief stated. Every Child Matters. It's that next generation that we have to start teaching. We are at all different levels as residential school survivors, all different levels of healing... A lot of parents forgot how to parent [and] grandparents forgot how to be grandparents. We need to start creating a new legacy, and it starts within the communities. It starts with the communities... Let's recognize that together as a people, not as First Nations and non-First Nations but as a people... that's how we have to do this...

- Chief Fred Robbins[10]

During the monument ceremonies, and other events, there were signs of Orange Shirt Day already. People were wearing "Every Child Matters" pins, the choir wore orange scarves and the committee handed out orange bags. It was a sign that Orange Shirt Day would become the medium for continuing the conversation about Residential Schools annually.

Musicians Gary Fjellgaard and Murray Porter each shared the songs they wrote after hearing Canada's 2008 federal apology for the Residential School System. They performed their songs during the commemoration project events.

Remembering, Recovering, and Reconciling

Tslluk'wmínstem, Ltwilc, ell Xyemstwécw
(Secwepemc)

Jinataghelnih, Sa?anataghdilh jilh
Chenaxedaghedelh
(Tsilhqot'in)

Whunats'ulnih, Soona'uts'utneh, Soo
hubulhninaowts'unt'ai
(Southern Dakelh/Carrier)

Today we dedicate ourselves to the
healing journey of all of those affected
by the St Joseph's Mission (Cariboo)
Residential School that operated on
this site from July 19, 1891 to
June 30, 1981.

"...the absence of an apology has
been an impediment to healing and
reconciliation. Therefore on behalf
of the Government of Canada and
all Canadians, I stand before you...
to apologize to Aboriginal peoples
for Canada's role in the Indian
Residential Schools system."
Prime Minister Stephen Harper
June 11, 2008

"...We deeply, and very
specifically, apologize to
every victim of (physical and
sexual) abuse and we seek
help in searching for means
to bring about healing."
Missionary Oblates of
Mary Immaculate
July 24, 1991

I APOLOGIZE
By Gary Fjellgaard

I have this guilt / I have this shame
I have a conscience / So I have to take the blame
I stood back / I watched it all
I even helped imprison you / Behind those walls
No excuse / Is good enough
We never let you speak / Unless you mimicked us
I can't run / I can't hide
Why I can't even / Look you in the eye
No hollow prayer / No silent shout
No more empty words / Spilling from my mouth
You stripped away / My thin disguise
Now all that I can do is say / I'm sorry
I apologize
I thought that God / Was on my side
And with my righteousness / I'd tame the savage child
I would not have them / Running free
If they assimilate / They could be like me
How many can / The wagons hold
Another thousand children / I suppose
It must have seemed / Like judgement day
The anguish / As the wagons rolled away
I can't begin / To know your pain
You can't forgive / As long as memory remains
Through it all / You still survive
And all that I can do is say / I'm sorry
Choking on the words that say / I'm sorry
I apologize

> *I wrote this song after hearing the federal government make their apology in 2008. My wife, Lynn, and I were driving and we were listening to CBC radio and listening to some of the accounts of survivors and victims and their families and we were moved not just to tears but... I think our soul was stirred. And that night, I wrote this song and I didn't have a clue what to do with it so I recorded it and put it on the website as a free download... I guess my wish is for everyone to hear that there are people like me who have to take the blame and I'm taking my share here.*

- Gary Fjellgaard[11]

nadian singer Gary Fjellgaard.

IS SORRY ENOUGH?

Written By: Elaine Bomberry and Murray Porter

Now you say you're sorry
It's not what you say
It's what you do
You tell us you'll do better
But it's hard to believe in you
The day has finally come
Told the world, you were wrong
Far too many have passed on now
When is sorry enough?
You took away our children
Stole their Mother's love
Laid waste to our traditions
Wasn't that enough?
Separated from our culture
So many years, so alone
With no Mothers and no Fathers
In a world so far from home
Forced to use another language
Punished when you spoke your Native tongue
You tried to kill our spirits
But our hearts still beat as one
I wasn't born to be here
City's not my home
It's not my Native land
But the streets are so familiar
This is not what our Mothers planned
You took away our children
Stole their Mother's love
Laid waste to our traditions
Wasn't that enough?
When will it be enough?
When is Sorry Enough?

...my name is Murray Porter and I am a Mohawk turtle clan of Six Nations of the Grand River Territory... I watched the [2008 Federal] apology with a box of Kleenex and a week later I wrote this song to talk about the apology from our perspective.

- Murray Porter [12]

A beaded orange shirt by Lynette La Fontaine for the Adult Day Center in Old Masset, Haida Gwaii in September 2018.

ST. JOSEPH'S MISSION RESIDENTIAL SCHOOL REUNION

After the week-long St. Joseph's Mission Commemoration and Monument Dedication, a reunion was held on the weekend of May 18-19, 2013 for the **Survivors**, their families and local communities. The reunion took place outdoors at the Chief Will-Yum Pow Wow Grounds and Campsite on T'exelc (Williams Lake Indian Band) Territory.[13] The goal of the reunion was to reunite old friends, make new ones and to have fun!

Organizers of the reunion planned on providing food for a maximum of 250 people; over 1200 people attended! Breaking the bannock in half did not even begin to help feed everyone! Luckily, Williams Lake city was a short 10 minute drive away for people to enjoy some food.

Both days began with a sunrise ceremony. There was entertainment throughout the weekend for both youth and adults. The game of competition lahal (stick games) was played with prizes for the top three teams. On Saturday, a special performance was given by Gary Fjellgaard and a *"Dance Under the Stars"* with music provided by an array of First Nation music bands.

Each day included an "open mike" for personal reflections from Survivors and their families. The reunion was a safe place to bond and share their stories. As survivors shared their truths of their experiences at The Mission, other attendees provided comfort and support.

Attendee Agnes Snow commented: [14]

> *"Sometimes we feel really bad about the things that happened to us. It's ok to do that, but don't get stuck there. It's not going to help the younger generation. We have to begin to heal. Nobody can do it for you. You have to do the work."*

A special ceremony was held to honour deceased St. Joseph Mission students by a representative of each of the four Nations that attended The Mission. These Nations included the Secwépemc (Shuswap), the Tsilhqot'in (Chilcotin), the Southern Dakelh (Carrier) and St'at'imc (Lillooet).

On Sunday, the reunion concluded with Indian bingo followed by closing remarks and closing ceremonies. Everyone was given a bag lunch for their journey back home. Many attendees expressed an interest in having future reunions.

Chief Fred Robbins speaks at the Reunion Ceremony concluding the Saint Joseph's Mission Commemoration Project events. Film still by John Dell.

Crowds at the Reunion Ceremony for the St. Joseph's Mission Commemoration Project events. Film still by John Dell.

Drummers at the Reunion Ceremony for the St. Joseph's Mission Commemoration Project events. Film still by John Dell.

ONGOING LEGACY

The efforts made by Chief Fred Robbins, the planning committee and the St. Joseph's Mission Residential School Commemoration Project have created a new legacy for Indigenous peoples in Canada. Because of Chief Fred's vision for reconciliation and the events that took place in 2013, reconciliation between Indigenous and non-Indigenous peoples in Canada has gained significant momentum.

Orange Shirt Day was born from these events. Phyllis Webstad's courage, sharing her story for the first time at the press conference, planted the seed that grew into Orange Shirt Day. In 2017, Phyllis Webstad received the Thompson River University Distinguished Alumni Community Impact Award for her unprecedented impact on local, provincial, national and international communities through the sharing of her orange shirt story.[15]

The expansion of Orange Shirt Day and the "Every Child Matters" campaign is one of the most impactful and unexpected results of the events that took place in Williams Lake in 2013. It is now widely understood that as Canadians it is our duty to educate ourselves and recognize our painful dark history and to commit to reconciliation, ensuring tragedies like Residential Schools never happen again.

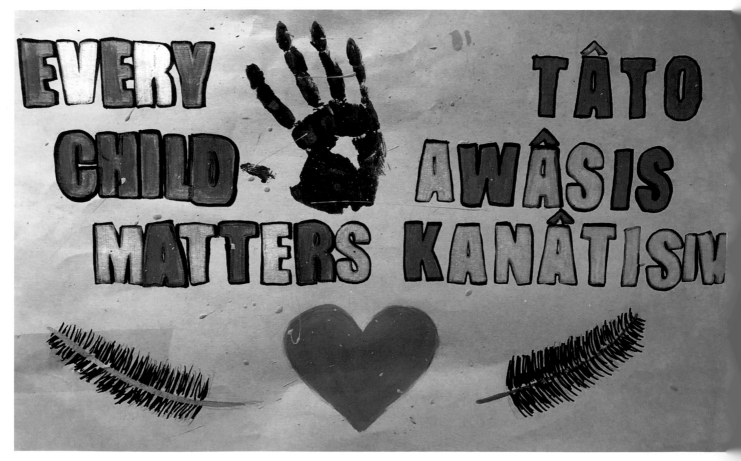

Artwork by Juniper Elementary School student Cherish Cooper. Cherish says, "my poster honours children that went to Residential School... I am Swampy Cree from Cross Lake First Nation. I decided to translate 'Every Child Matters' into my language."

In 2013, Al Richmond, former Chair of the Cariboo Regional District, gifts Chief Fred Robbins with the Key to the Cariboo for his efforts with reconciliation. Witnessed by Mike Archie and others. Film still by John Dell.

Al Richmond, former Chair of the Cariboo Regional District, presented Chief Fred Robbins with the Key to the Cariboo Award for his vision for reconciliation and his work in making the project come to fruition. Al Richmond proclaimed, "on behalf of the residents of the Carboo Chilcotin, and every member of our board, we would like you to take this gift, as a token of our appreciation for what you've brought forward for your people. And, hopefully it's the beginning of us having wonderful first steps in how we bring forward our communities so we can be a better place to live, work and play." [16] Chief Fred was given the British Columbia Achievement Award in 2017 as well as the 2013 Community Excellence Award Presented by the Union of British Columbia Municipalities.[17]

Chief Fred Robbins' passion to bring Indigenous and non-Indigenous people together to acknowledge the painful truths of Residential Schools and begin the recovery process had become a reality that inspired national change and healing for many.

The Orange Shirt Society thanks Chief Fred for starting the community on a path to reconciliation.

CHAPTER FOUR QUESTIONS

REVIEW

1. In May, 2013, there was a series of reconciliation events that took place. Who did it involve and what was the main goal? Where did these events take place?

2. Whose vision inspired so many people to work towards reconciliation in May, 2013?

3. 3.) What was Chief Justice Murray Sinclair's challenge to the participants of these reconciliation events?

4. Complete the following sentences from Chief Fred Robbins' quote. "We're ready to move _____ and build _____; to build a new _____ for First Nations people, not built on _____."

5. How did Chief Fred Robbins' vision of reconciliation involve an epitaph? How did he believe this to be important?

6. What was the St. Joseph's Mission Residential School Commemoration Project?

7. What was the theme that emerged during the planning of the project for St. Joseph's Mission Residential School Commemoration Project?

8. At what event did Phyllis Webstad first share the story of her orange shirt?

9. What year did Phyllis Webstad attend Residential School? For how long?

10. Phyllis Webstad mentioned that she was not the first generation of people from her family to attend a Residential School. How many generations of her family attended Residential Schools?

11. What inspired musicians Murray Porter and Gary Fjellgaard to write their songs?

ACTIVITY

In this chapter you had the chance to read lyrics by Gary Fjellgaard and Murray Porter. Both musicians were inspired, in their own way, from Canada's Apology from 2008. Read or watch Canada's apology online. Refer to our online resource page at www.medicinewheel.education/orangeshirtday.

Can you come up with your own way of sharing how you feel about Canada's apology? This could be a poem, song, artwork or any other form of expression.

REFLECT

1. Chief Fred's goal for this project was reconciliation. Why do you think he needed both Indigenous and non-Indigenous people to participate in order to achieve reconciliation?

2. During the St. Joseph's Residential School Commemoration Project events there were many opportunities where Survivors could tell their truth of what took place in Residential Schools. Why is truth telling a pre-requisite to reconciliation?

3. What was former Mayor Kerry Cook's response to Chief Fred Robbins' vision?

RESEARCH

Visit our Online Resources at www.medicinewheel.education. There you will find links for Gary Fjellgaard's song *I Apologize* and Murray Porter's song *Is Sorry Enough*.

SOURCES

1. Webstad, Phyllis. Personal Interview. January. 2020.
2. "Chief Fred Robbins Speech." Boitanio Park Monument Unveiling. The Commemoration Project Events. Filmed by John Dell. Signal Point Media, 2013. DVD.
3. Tarbell, Harold. St. Joseph's Mission Residential School Commemoration Project Document. Remembering, Recovering, and Reconciling. Williams Lake: Tarbell Facilitation Network, 2013.
4. Tarbell, Harold. St. Joseph's Mission Residential School Commemoration Project Document. Remembering, Recovering, and Reconciling. Williams Lake: Tarbell Facilitation Network, 2013.
5. Moses, Tiffany. St. Joseph's Mission Residential School Commemoration Project Brochure. Remembering, Recovering, and Reconciling. Williams Lake: Tarbell Facilitation Network, 2013.
6. Cook, Kerry. Personal Interview. March. 2020.
7. Webstad, Phyllis. Personal Interview. January. 2020
8. Phyllis Webstad Shares her Orange Shirt Story for the First Time." Commemoration Project Event Press Conference. Filmed by John Dell. Signal Point Media, 2013. Film.
9. Webstad, Phyllis. Joan Sorley, Tiffany Moses and Harold Tarbell. St. Joseph's Mission Residential School Commemoration Project Booklet. Remembering, Recovering, and Reconciling. Williams Lake: Tarbell Facilitation Network, 2013. pp. 12.
10. "Chief Fred Robbins Speech." Boitanio Park Monument Unveiling. The Commemoration Project Events. Filmed by John Dell. Signal Point Media, 2013. DVD.
11. "Gary Fjellgaard Speech." Boitanio Park Monument Unveiling. The Commemoration Project Events. Filmed by John Dell. Signal Point Media, 2013. DVD.
12. "Murray Porter Speech." Boitanio Park Monument Unveiling. The Commemoration Project Events. Filmed by John Dell. Signal Point Media, 2013. DVD.
13. Tarbell, Harold. St. Joseph's Mission Residential School Commemoration Project Document. Remembering, Recovering, and Reconciling. Williams Lake: Tarbell Facilitation Network, 2013.
14. Tarbell, Harold. St. Joseph's Mission Residential School Commemoration Project Document. Remembering, Recovering, and Reconciling. Williams Lake: Tarbell Facilitation Network, 2013.
15. "2017 Recipients." Thompson River University. <https://www.tru.ca/alumni/distinguished_alumni_awards/2017_Recipients_Distinguished_Alumni.html> accessed May 5, 2020.
16. "Chief Fred Ribbons is Gifted the Key to Cariboo." Truth and Reconciliation Commission. The Commemoration Project Events. Filmed by John Dell. Signal Point Media, 2013. DVD.
17. "Former Chief Fred Robbins Named BC Achievement Award Recipient." Williams Lake Tribune. April 1, 2017. <https://www.wltribune.com/news/former-chief-fred-robbins-named-bc-achievement-award-recipient/> accessed May 29, 2020.

"AFN National Chief Congratulates Esket'emc First Nation for Winning a 2013 Community Excellence Award…" Assembly of First Nations. September 19, 2013. <https://www.afn.ca/afn-national-chief-congratulates-esketemc-first-nation-for-winning-a-2/> accessed May 29, 2020.

Orange Shirt Day at the University of Victoria in 2018. Photo courtesy of UVIC Photo Services.

5 ORANGE SHIRT DAY
AND THE ORANGE SHIRT SOCIETY

Orange Shirt Day is a legacy of the St. Joseph's Mission Residential School Commemoration Project. Since its creation, Orange Shirt Day has become a movement that inspires Indian Residential School reconciliation and has created safe spaces for Survivors, and their families, to bravely share their experiences.

Orange Shirt Day acknowledges the Residential School tragedies and, in turn, creates opportunities for collective and individual healing, recovery and reconciliation. Since the first Orange Shirt Day, on September 30, 2013, many people have begun to awaken to this shameful chapter in our history and the importance of establishing a new legacy for Indigenous people that says, "Every Child Matters."

Shawn Atleo, former National Assembly of First Nations Chief from 2009 to 2014, at the first Orange Shirt Day in 2013 at Boitanio Park in Williams Lake. Photo courtesy of the Williams Lake CRD.

Phyllis Webstad surrounded by her family at an Orange Shirt Day event. Left to right: Phyllis's mother Rose Wilson, husband Shawn Webstad, father John Butt and Aunt Agness Jack. Photo by Monica Lamb-Yorski of the Williams Lake Tribune.

Joan Sorley and Phyllis Webstad at the Williams Lake 2019 Orange Shirt Day event. Photo by Monica Lamb-Yorski of the Williams Lake Tribune.

HOW IT ALL BEGAN

As the St. Joseph's Mission Residential School Commemoration Project was about to begin its series of reconciliation events, a press conference was held to launch 'kick off week'; at this press conference Phyllis Webstad was encouraged, by her friend Joan Sorley, to share her Residential School experience at St. Joseph's Mission and the story of her orange shirt. Sharing her story was not an easy decision as her experience at Residential School had impacted her entire life.

Phyllis explained how difficult it was to wear the colour orange. The colour brought up feelings of low self-worth due to the trauma she experienced as a child at Residential School. *"As a result, orange came to symbolize for her that nobody cared that she had feelings and that she just didn't matter and how it led to her growing up thinking she wasn't worth anything."* [1] Phyllis's orange shirt represents the triumphant reclamation of her identity, self worth and hope for the future.

Many other Survivors connect with her story because they too had similar experiences of their identity and belongings being taken away. Ultimately, Phyllis's story is a conversation starter about all aspects of Residential Schools and the way that the system negatively affected individuals and families, both first-hand and generationally.

Phyllis' story was so powerful and relatable, not only to other Survivors and their families, but to everyone. Many felt it greatly represented not only the trauma inflicted by Residential Schools but also the pain felt afterwards and the long journey of healing and recovery.

THE FIRST ORANGE SHIRT DAY

After Phyllis shared her story at the press conference in April of 2013, the idea for Orange Shirt Day was born.

We wanted to find a way to not let the conference be the end… but rather the beginning of ongoing conversations around the devastating impacts of Residential Schools. I thought, wait a minute… we have Pink Shirt Day and Remembrance Day why don't we have an Orange Shirt Day, so we can have at least one day where we talk about these hard topics every year.

- Joan Sorley[2]

After all events were completed around the St. Joseph's Mission Residential School Commemoration Project, the planning committee morphed into the Orange Shirt Society.

The annual Orange Shirt Day on September 30th opens the door to global conversation on all aspects of Residential Schools. It is an opportunity to create meaningful discussion about the effects of Residential Schools and the legacy they have left behind. A discussion all Canadians can tune into and create bridges with each other for reconciliation. A day for survivors to be reaffirmed that they matter, and so do those that have been affected. Every Child Matters, even if they are an adult, from now on.

- Phyllis Webstad[3]

As word about Phyllis's story and Orange Shirt Day began to spread, people wanted to become involved and begin walking the path of reconciliation. Prior to the first Orange Shirt Day, Shannon Bell, a pastor in the community of Ndazkoh B.C., witnessed Phyllis share her orange shirt story at a TRC event in May of 2013. She was inspired by Phyllis's courage and recognized the importance of creating momentum for Orange Shirt Day. Shannon quickly took action to become involved and share Phyllis's story.

"In May 2013 I attended the regional TRC event in Williams Lake with a friend who is an Indian Residential School Survivor and former Chief of our community. We listened to Phyllis Webstad share her story of her beloved orange shirt and the plans to mark September 30 as Orange Shirt Day in the city of Williams Lake and School District 27. I was moved by her story and taken with the idea of having a day to acknowledge the Survivors of Residential Schools and remember those who did not survive. Following Phyllis' presentation… I said to our local superintendent, 'We need to bring this to Quesnel schools as well!' I felt that Phyllis' story made the issue of Residential Schools relatable to everyone.

A couple of days later I phoned Phyllis and thanked her for sharing her story and for the idea of Orange Shirt Day. I explained that I didn't want to interfere or overstep, but asked if she would be comfortable with me trying to expand the reach of the idea to a wider audience. I wanted to try to make Orange Shirt Day go viral. In preparation for the national TRC event, I printed 5,000 hand-outs about Orange Shirt Day to distribute to everyone possible that we met at the event. I and others [including five Survivors] handed out the small flyers to everyone we met.

After returning home, I turned over the administration of the Facebook page and website to Phyllis and stepped back from any visible role. My goal had been to promote Phyllis and her story so that more people would hear the truth of the history of IRS's and their continued impact on our Indigenous neighbours… I'm so pleased to have played a small part in getting the word out so that people can begin to create bridges of reconciliation… I was excited to see that the pages began to have traffic and exposure first locally and eventually across the country and world. The first comment we received from overseas was from a supporter in Italy!" [4]

Orange Shirt Day
September 30

Wear an orange shirt to honour the children who survived the Indian Residential Schools and to remember those who didn't.

For more info visit:
www.facebook.com/wearorangeshirt
or
www.ndazkohpastor.wix.com/orangeshirtday
Pass it on!

Shannon Bell photographed by her husband Jon Wyminga.

Orange Shirt Day 2017 at Bellerose Composite High School in Alberta. Photo by Michael Larocque.

The very first Orange Shirt Day was on September 30th, 2013 and events were held across Canada and beyond. At these events, Indigenous and non-Indigenous local communities came together to support the creation of a new legacy for Indigenous peoples.

The first Orange Shirt Day turned out to be much bigger than initially expected. The day was organized by Phyllis Webstad, David DeRose, Joan Sorley, Jerome Beauchamp, and Anne Burrill for the Williams Lake and 100 Mile House communities.

WHY SEPTEMBER 30th

The date of September 30th was chosen very carefully. This date represented the time of year when the Indigenous children were collected from their homes, forced to leave their families and attend Residential Schools. September 30th was chosen to allow schools and teachers to settle into their school year, teach the students about Residential Schools and to plan an event for Orange Shirt Day. Additionally, by having Orange Shirt Day at the beginning of the school year, it sets the stage for anti-racism and anti-bullying policies to inspire inclusion.

"While listening to the truths at the September, 2013, TRC event in Vancouver I overheard an Elder say that September was crying month. It was then that I knew that we had chosen the right day for Orange Shirt Day."

- Phyllis Webstad [5]

Lucy Squalian and carver Dean Gilpin pose in front of one of the commemorative monuments, showing Dean's artwork, in Williams Lake. Photo is by Valerie West.

WHY THE MESSAGE "EVERY CHILD MATTERS"

"Every Child Matters" is the chosen theme and one of the core guiding principles for the Orange Shirt Society. It was chosen in response to Phyllis feeling that she did not matter. This message reminds Survivors that they are important and they matter. "Every Child Matters" extends beyond Residential School Survivors and their families, to include all children. "Every Child Matters" also includes those children who died at, or as a result of, Residential Schools.

"Every Child Matters" is for all children past, present and future. All children in Canada and beyond. All those who were children. All those who suffered as children at Residential School who became adults and those that didn't. When the Orange Shirt Society says "Every Child Matters"... it means everyone, including you who are reading this, regardless of background or age.

"Imagine a world where any child can grow up feeling like they matter."

- Jerome Beauchamp, President of Orange Shirt Society[6]

Every Child Matters

#ORANGESHIRTDAY

Nanestsen (I care for you)

"In this image, I depict a contemporary young First Nations woman holding a girl in a Residential School uniform, she holds her close in a way that conveys both love and protection. The girl's hair is short due to mandatory regulations at Residential School that forced children to have their hair cut. The young woman has kept her hair long and braided and while she's dressed in contemporary fashion she also chooses to wear moccasins and beaded earrings. I wanted to show that First Nations and Indigenous people have endured the harm experienced at Residential Schools through multi-generational resilience. As time moves forward, we remain tethered to our ancestors who experienced this harm and I wonder about the space, compassion and understanding we can share with our relations both in the present and our past."
Artwork by Karlene Harvey. [7]

ORANGE SHIRT DAY AND INTERGENERATIONAL TRAUMA

Orange Shirt Day has inspired many people and events to honour Residential School Survivors, their families and the children who didn't come home. Through this day, and the movement towards reconciliation that it has inspired, people are beginning to understand and acknowledge the painful truths that have impacted individuals, families and communities.

By sharing the effects of Phyllis Webstad's intergenerational trauma, Phyllis has shown us how difficult it is to overcome the long-lasting pain caused by Residential Schools. One of the most powerful outcomes of Orange Shirt Day is that it has inspired people to share their first-hand and intergenerational experiences with Residential Schools.

> *I was 13.8 years old and in grade eight when my son Jeremy was born. Because my grandmother and mother both attended Residential School for ten years each, I never knew what a parent was supposed to be like. With the help of my aunt, Agness Jack, I was able to raise my son and have him know me as his mother.*
>
> *I went to a treatment centre for healing when I was 27 and have been on this healing journey since then. I finally get it, that the feeling of worthlessness and insignificance, ingrained in me from my first day at the Mission, affected the way I lived my life for many years. Even now, when I know nothing could be further than the truth, I still sometimes feel that I don't matter. Even with all the work I've done!*

-Phyllis Webstad[8]

These shared stories have emphasized a collective truth amongst Indigenous peoples that can no longer be ignored. Through the acknowledgement of these shared truths, the process of healing and recovery can be widely embraced creating reconciliation among Indigenous and non-Indigenous people.

Phyllis Webstad reading from her book *Phyllis's Orange Shirt* at Orange Shirt Day 2019 in Williams Lake. Photo by Monica Lamb-Yorski of the Williams Lake Tribune.

THE ORANGE SHIRT SOCIETY

The Orange Shirt Society is a non-profit organization created by a group of volunteers, from the St. Joseph's Mission Commemoration Project, who are committed to the development of Orange Shirt Day. The Society is located in Williams Lake B.C., where Phyllis Webstad first shared her story about her orange shirt and attended St. Joseph's Mission Residential School. The Society was formed as a way to organize Orange Shirt Day, create events and spread awareness. Orange Shirt Society has three purposes that aid in the development and awareness of Orange Shirt Day: [9]

- To support Indian Residential School Reconciliation

- To create awareness of the individual, family and community intergenerational impacts of Indian Residential Schools through Orange Shirt Society activities

- To create awareness of the concept of "Every Child Matters"

The Orange Shirt Society is directed by a board of both Indigenous and non-Indigenous volunteers. The founding members of the Orange Shirt Society are Phyllis Webstad, David DeRose, Joan Sorley, Jerome Beauchamp, Margo Wagner, Margaret Anne-Enders and Anne Burrill.

Phyllis Webstad, Joan Sorley and Jerome Beauchamp celebrate the official Orange Shirt Society office opening in 2019 in Williams Lake, B.C. Photo by Monica Lamb-Yorski of the Williams Lake Tribune.

Phyllis Webstad admiring student artwork at Desert Sands Community School, Ashcroft, B.C. presentation in 2019.

It took Phyllis nearly 40 years to wear the colour orange again after the Residential School took away her orange shirt. Now she, and the Orange Shirt Society, have bravely transformed her painful experience into a movement that represents Residential School reconciliation and healing. What was once a symbol of pain and tragedy for Phyllis, is now a symbol of hope. Phyllis now wears orange shirts to symbolize that "Every Child Matters," including her and you.

You too can wear an orange shirt on September 30th to send the message that "Every Child Matters." Wearing orange also shows that you acknowledge and support the healing journey of Indigenous people who are courageously recovering from the effects of Residential Schools and building a new legacy for themselves, their families, and communities.

The government that did this to us will never go to jail for what they did. Whenever I see someone wearing an orange shirt and witness children in schools learning about what happened to us, it feels like a little bit of justice in our lifetime."

- Phyllis Webstad [10]

THE FUTURE OF ORANGE SHIRT DAY

Orange Shirt Day has expanded across Canada and beyond. Initially envisioned as an opportunity to hold tough conversations about what happened in Residential Schools in the Cariboo Region of British Columbia, it has now become a widely recognized movement for reconciliation. Orange Shirt Day is not only a day to honour Survivors and their families but it is also an opportunity for people of all ages and backgrounds to become educated about Residential Schools and the process of reconciliation while promoting "Every Child Matters."

Social media has been an incredible asset for spreading the message and awareness about Orange Shirt Day. The Orange Shirt Society has seen every photo and post on both Instagram and Facebook! The Society has seen your school group photos, your heart-shaped group photos, your pins, your crafts and your handmade orange shirts. The Society encourages you to continue sharing your Orange Shirt Day efforts and commemorations by posting on social media with the hashtag #orangeshirtday.

Orange Shirt Day has been nationally recognized and embraced. Phyllis Webstad and Joan Sorley were present in the House of Commons March 21, 2019, for the historic occasion of the third reading of Bill C-369, which would have made September 30th a federal statutory holiday. Unfortunately, although it passed that day in the House, it didn't make it through the Senate before Parliament dissolved in advance of the 2019 federal election.[11] It is unknown if the Canadian Government will revive it.

Orange Shirt Day has also inspired wide-spread curriculum change within Canadian schools in order to include the truths of Residential Schools and Indigenous cultural genocide. It is the Society's dream that this day will be used to further the education of Residential Schools and reconciliation, and to honour all those affected by Residential Schools as stated in Call to Action #80 from the Truth and Reconciliation Commission of Canada.[12]

Executive director of the Orange Shirty Society, Phyllis Webstad and board member Joan Sorley were invited by Heritage Ministry of Canada on March 21st, 2019, to witness the passing of Bill C-369 in parliament in Ottawa. Photo taken by Joan Sorley.

Children marching for Orange Shirt Day in Shulus, B.C. Photo taken by Dara Hill of the Merritt Herald.

CHAPTER FIVE QUESTIONS

REVIEW

1. When was the first Orange Shirt Day?

2. What is the central message of Orange Shirt Day and the Orange Shirt Society?

3. After the events were completed for the St. Joseph's Mission Residential School Commemoration Project what did the planning committee morph into?

4. Shannon Bell was inspired to help spread the message about the first Orange Shirt Day. How many printed hand-outs did she and her helpers give out and where?

5. What date was chosen to be Orange Shirt Day? Why was this date chosen?

6. Who is the Orange Shirt Society referring to when they say "Every Child Matters?"

7. How many purposes does the Orange Shirt Society have? Please list each purpose.

8. What are you acknowledging by wearing an Orange Shirt on Orange Shirt Day?

9. Fill in the blank. What was once a symbol of pain and tragedy for Phyllis, is now a symbol of _____.

ACTIVITY

Write a letter to all Canadians answering the following questions:

- Briefly answer what took place in the Residential School system in Canada.
- Why should all Canadians be concerned with Indigenous rights?
- Explain Phyllis's story to them and why her story is important for all Canadians to understand.
- What would the future of the world look like if every child were treated like they mattered?

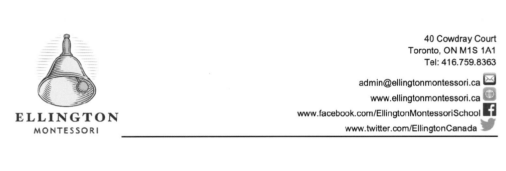

40 Cowdray Court
Toronto, ON M1S 1A1
Tel: 416.759.8363

admin@ellingtonmontessori.ca
www.ellingtonmontessori.ca
www.facebook.com/EllingtonMontessoriSchool
www.twitter.com/EllingtonCanada

ELLINGTON
MONTESSORI

Dear Ms. Webstad,

Ms. Webstad, it is a privilege to be writing to you. I have learned about Orange Day during the classroom discussion about the residential schools and that encouraged me to know more about your story. I was overwhelmed to find out what you went through at St. Joseph Mission Residential School. Ms. Webstad, it must have been hard to be living in such a traumatic state of mind, at such a young age.

I think the era of residential schooling was one of the darkest spans of Canadian history. It must have been an awful experience when the young children were deprived of being with their families, following their tradition and even something as basic as eating what they like. My heart goes out to all the 150, 000 students at residential schools at that time who were abused physically, mentally and emotionally. It must have been an unimaginable extent of suffering.

This year, in my school, the elementary students performed a skit. The skit revolved around the incident when your grandma hands over an orange shirt to you and how brutally it was taken away. While we were playing the characters it felt like we were living those moments ourselves. On the other hand, we have been fortunate enough to have one of the residential school survivors among us as a guest of honour. She was in tears throughout our performance. Later, Elder Chaboyer began to share her own experience of the residential school she went to and it left us speechless.

The story of suppression does not end here. Unfortunately, it still continues when a child is bullied, when one is taken for granted, when one is not treated well, when one is made to feel unworthy, it is very disheartening to go through these emotions especially as a child.

However, there is always a light at the end of the tunnel. Ms. Webstad, I have learnt a lot through your story. You inspire me to be patient through the tough times and face the rainy days. Also it made me realize we, as children, are privileged to be living with our families, go to a school that we like, to be able to play and talk with our friends and more such; things in our lives we are grateful for. Thank you for choosing to share your story that in a way has been a catalyst to encourage the younger generation.

Yours sincerely,

Josephine, Somasundaram

Grade – five

REFLECTION

1. What do you think are appropriate terms to use when referring to Orange Shirt Day? Celebrate? Honour? Remember? Which do you think are honouring the day appropriately considering the context of the Orange Shirt Day?

2. Shannon Bell was inspired to spread awareness of Orange Shirt Day by tapping into her creative and social skillset. What skills and resources do you have that could benefit a movement like Orange Shirt Day?

3. An Orange Shirt has become a symbol. What do you think it symbolizes for Indigenous Survivors of Residential Schools, like Phyllis Webstad? Please write what you think it symbolizes to those affected in your own words.

RESEARCH

Is there a new bill to make September 30th a statutory holiday?

SOURCES

1. Tarbell, Harold. St. Joseph's Mission Residential School Commemoration Project Document. Remembering, Recovering, and Reconciling. Williams Lake: Tarbell Facilitation Network, 2013.
2. Sorley, Joan. Personal Interview. January. 2020.
3. Webstad, Phyllis. Personal Interview. January. 2020.
4. Bell, Shannon, personal interview. March. 2020
5. Webstad, Phyllis. Personal Interview. January. 2020.
6. Beauchamp, Jerome. Personal Interview. November. 2020.
7. Harvey, Karlene. Personal Interview. April. 2020.
8. Webstad, Phyllis. Personal Interview. January. 2020.
9. "Orange Shirt Society." Orange Shirt Day. <https://www.orangeshirtday.org/orange-shirt-society.html> accessed May 1, 2020.
10. Webstad, Phyllis. Personal Interview. January. 2020.
11. "Today Might Have Been a Stat Holiday - if it Wasn't Election Time." National Post. September 30, 2019. <https://nationalpost.com/news/canada/today-might-have-been-a-stat-holiday-if-it-wasnt-election-timehttps://nationalpost.com/news/canada/today-might-have-been-a-stat-holiday-if-it-wasnt-election-time> accessed May 15, 2020.
12. "Truth and Reconciliation Commission of Canada: Calls to Action." Truth and Reconciliation Commission of Canada. 2015. <http://trc.ca/assets/pdf/Calls_to_Action_English2.pdf> accessed February 1, 2020. pp. 9.

6 HOW TO PARTICIPATE IN ORANGE SHIRT DAY

Participating in Orange Shirt Day on September 30th can motivate massive and positive change collectively, nationally and individually. Through your participation you will contribute to creating a new legacy for Indigenous peoples. Your participation can include becoming educated on the history of Residential Schools in Canada and reconciliation as well as holding space for Survivors and their families to share their truths. Your participation and education will also help you to confront **racism**, stereotypes and prejudices against Indigenous people. Orange Shirt Day has the power to create a more inclusive future by inspiring reconciliation, broader education, new perspectives and societal change.

Orange Shirt Day is not just a day on September 30th, it is a year-around educational movement designed to raise awareness of the continuing impacts of Residential School and promote reconciliation. By participating and becoming an advocate for this movement, you are changing culture on local, national and personal levels. By investing your time, energy and resources into Orange Shirt Day you are creating a more educated, supportive and inclusive environment that truly believes "Every Child Matters."

There are many ways that you can participate in Orange Shirt Day. There is no limit on your involvement when it comes to creating a positive and rightful new legacy for Indigenous peoples. As you become educated on the history and pain of Residential Schools, you may also create new and groundbreaking ways to participate in Orange Shirt Day.

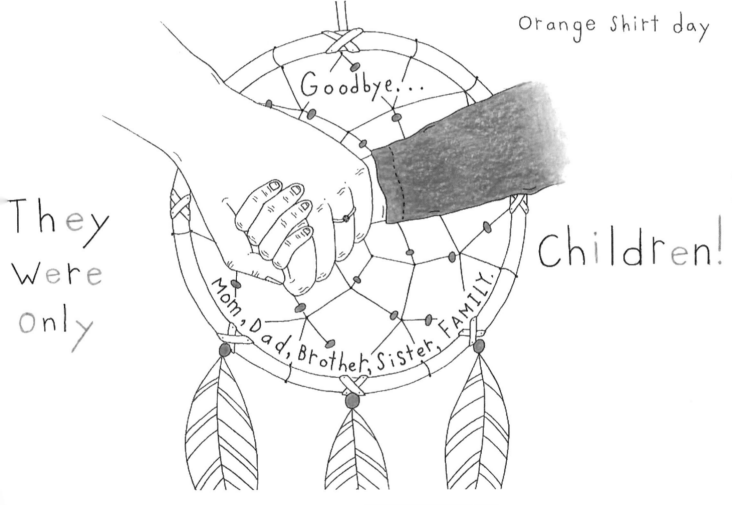

Artwork by grade 7 student Norah Melnyk

WEARING AN ORANGE SHIRT

The most obvious way to participate in Orange Shirt Day is to wear an orange shirt on September 30th! You can create your own shirt, or buy an official one through the Orange Shirt Society's website at www.orangeshirtday.org. The Orange Shirt Society asks that your shirt reflect the message that "Every Child Matters." Here are a few ideas:

- Write "Every Child Matters" on your shirt
- Wear an official Orange Shirt Day pin, designed by Tiffany Moses
- Write what reconciliation means to you on your shirt
- Draw children's hands on your shirt to symbolize "Every Child Matters"

Creating your own orange shirt can be a great and social way to participate in Orange Shirt Day. You could make one on your own while reflecting on the reasons for your participation, or you could create one with friends and family while discussing your participation in reconciliation. If you choose to buy an official shirt or pin, you can do so on the Orange Shirt Society website (www.orangeshirtday.org) where a portion of the proceeds go back to the Society. There are other vendors selling orange shirts for Orange Shirt Day, but very few support the Orange Shirt Society and its work.

Whether you choose to make your orange shirt or purchase it, there are a few things to consider. It is important that your orange shirt says "Every Child Matters" because it's central to the purpose of Orange Shirt Society. If you don't have an orange shirt, can't afford one, or don't want to write on your shirt, anything orange will do! It's the conversation that's important.

Vancity staff pose for Orange Shirt Day 2018. Vancity is a founding partner of Reconciliation Canada. Photo taken by Paulina Tsui.

Phyllis Webstad accompanied on stage by her mother, Rose Wilson, and Al Richmond at an Orange Shirt Day event. Photo by Monica Lamb-Yorski of the Williams Lake Tribune.

HOW TO SHARE PHYLLIS WEBSTAD'S STORY

Phyllis Webstad's hope is that you will share the story of her orange shirt and begin to educate yourself, and others, on Residential Schools and the experiences of Indigenous peoples in Canada. You can learn about Phyllis's story in this book, online or through the two children's books she wrote detailing her orange shirt story.

The Orange Shirt Story is written for ages seven and up, and *Phyllis's Orange Shirt* is written for ages four to six. Both books are illustrated by Brock Nicol and are available in English and French, with *The Orange Shirt Story* also available in Shuswap. *The Orange Shirt Story* was the #1 selling children's book in Canada in September 2018[1]. *Phyllis's Orange Shirt* was a B.C. Best Seller in September 2019[2]. *Beyond the Orange Shirt Story*, designed for middle and high schools, will be available in 2021 to share more of Phyllis's story for young adult audiences.

For more Orange Shirt Day resources please vist:
www.medicinewheel.education/orangeshirtday

Books written by Phyllis Webstad and illustrated by Brock Nicol.

BECOME AN ADVOCATE

As an advocate for Orange Shirt Day you are publicly supporting Residential School reconciliation and creating awareness. As an advocate, you can share the impacts of Residential Schools and the intergenerational trauma that is still heavily felt. When your voice is heard you create the awareness that "Every Child Matters" and that there is critical need to build a new legacy for Indigenous peoples.

Another way that you can be an advocate for Orange Shirt Day is to support the goals of the Orange Shirt Society and actively share their message for change. As a reminder, these are the purposes of the Orange Shirt Society:[3]

- To support Indian Residential School Reconciliation
- To create awareness of the individual, family and community intergenerational impacts of Indian Residential Schools through Orange Shirt Society activities
- To create awareness of the concept of "Every Child Matters"

Being an advocate for Orange Shirt Day is also an act of personal reconciliation. Your actions and involvement will inevitably create change within yourself, that will inspire your own neighbours and community. As you take on this commitment of being an advocate, you set an example for others to create a more respectful and inclusive society.

BECOME EDUCATED...
THEN EDUCATE!

"Education is what got us into this mess — the use of education at least in terms of Residential Schools — but education is the key to reconciliation... We need to look at the way we are educating children. That's why we say that this is not an Aboriginal problem. It's a Canadian problem."

- Murray Sinclair [4]

As you become more educated on this dark chapter of our history you can begin to share that information with others. We recommend that you seek out educational materials on Residential Schools, Survivor stories and the process of reconciliation. Through your education, you will understand the importance of changing the education system in Canada so that Canada's traumatic history is not hidden. In order to create change, we must be equipped with the truths of the past.

When teachers and adults take initiatives to educate themselves on these topics, children become more aware of how they can be forces for positive change. As you become educated on the history of our past and the mistreatment of Indigenous peoples in Canada, you can make informed choices on how to create a new legacy and inspire reconciliation.

Please refer to our online resource page at
www.medicinewheel.education/orangeshirtday

EVERY CHILD MATTERS Wear Orange

BECAUSE EVERY CHILD MATTE

EVERY CHILD M

EVERY CHILD MATTERS

I.R.S.S
"Every Child Matters"
Honour survivours of the
Indian Residential School System

EVERY
CHILD
MATTERS
Wear ORANGE
friday, September 30th!

SCHOOLS

If you are a school or educational institution, there are many opportunities to support Indian Residential School reconciliation by participating in Orange Shirt Day activities. From Kindergarten to University, students rally on a yearly basis to raise awareness of the impacts of Residential Schools on Survivors, their families and their communities.

Here are some suggestions:

• Invite an Elder to your school to speak about Residential Schools and their impacts. Please ensure that you host the Elder with generosity, kindness and respect. Part of showing respect is following the traditional protocol of the area in which you reside. Please consult with local Indigenous communities or your Indigenous educational consultant to learn how to do that in a respectful way.

• Attend a public Orange Shirt Day event if there is one in your community

• Host your own Orange Shirt Day. This could include, but is not limited to, sharing Phyllis's story, reading her books and watching videos online.

• Decorating orange shirts to wear on September 30th

Orange Shirt Society speaker Phyllis Webstad is available, on a limited basis, to offer presentations to schools, universities and corporations across the country, both in-person and virtually. The Orange Shirt Society is working on developing a network of speakers and video presentations to create new educational opportunities.

For more resources, please visit www.orangeshirtday.org, and explore the resource tab. Also visit the events tab to explore what others are doing to observe Orange Shirt Day.

CREATE ARTWORK

During the month of September, countless classrooms and students passionately create art that represents Orange Shirt Day and what they've learned about Indian Residential School Reconciliation.

Popular topics include:

- Using orange shirt cutouts and writing "Every Child Matters"
- Writing "Every Child Matters" on hearts and placing the hearts around the school
- Writing exercises on "what reconciliation means to you" and "How I am participating in Orange Shirt Day"
- Decorating orange shirts to wear on September 30th

Creating art is a positive and cathartic way to express how one is affected by an experience or subject. Using art to express how Residential Schools and reconciliation affects you can inspire the journey of others and provoke thoughtful conversation. As well, creating artwork is a form of personal reconciliation because it helps you to process knowledge, thoughts, emotions and life-events that affect you in any way.

In the fall of 2019, Medicine Wheel Education along with the Orange Shirt Society hosted an art contest that saw hundreds of kids from around Canada submit artwork and writing pieces that detailed what Orange Shirt Day and Residential School reconciliation means to them. Throughout this book you will see many of the incredible pieces submitted to us! While it was not possible to feature every piece received, the Orange Shirt Society saw every piece and thanks those who took the time to participate in this project and share their personal experiences.

GET TO KNOW INDIGENOUS RESOURCES

Explore the different Indigenous resources within your community. These resources may vary from youth mentorship programs, therapeutic services, cultural studies classes, local history books, plant medicine teachings or local calls to action. There is a wide variety of Indigenous resources available to you, and as the passion for Residential School reconciliation broadens more resources will be created.

Additionally, if you find you require crisis support, at any time, there are helpline numbers available in the introduction of this book. For other educational resources please refer to www.medicinewheel.education/orangeshirtday.

ACKNOWLEDGE THE TRADITIONAL TERRITORY

Educate yourself as to the traditional territory on which you are situated. To show respect and as an act of reconciliation, ensure you acknowledge the traditional territory at the beginning of any gathering or assembly in the proper protocol of the territory.

Brothers Christopher N. and David N. at an Orange Shirt Day event in Toronto 2019. Photo taken by Nadya Kwandibens of Red Works Photography.

BE FLEXIBLE

Learning about Residential Schools, Survivor stories and reconciliation can be challenging because it involves the process of **unlearning** old ways of thinking. In the past, history books have not always included the facts and tragic details about Residential Schools and acts of cultural genocide.

Now, with the Orange Shirt Day movement and reconciliation, we have an opportunity to re-educate ourselves. Through this re-education, or re-learning, we can become fully aware of how the past impacts our future.

Being flexible means being willing to look at the past, present and future from a new perspective.

Unlearning is the process of discarding or overriding learned habits, lessons and concepts.

BUSINESSES

If you have a business, consider using your space to share information on Orange Shirt Day, Residential School reconciliation and the goals of the Orange Shirt Society. Here are several ways you can share these messages as a local business:

- Put posters or calls for action on your bulletin boards
- Stock local Indigenous history books and Phyllis Webstad's Orange Shirt Story books
- Display the Orange Shirt Day logo that says, "Every Child Matters"
- Allow your business to become an advocate for social change and Indigenous injustices in Canada

WRITE A LETTER

Write a letter to your local, provincial or national government encouraging greater efforts for reconciliation and awareness of Orange Shirt Day. As you educate yourself on your reconciliation resources, you may become aware of what actions need to take place to create change. By using your voice to call for action, you are actively participating in helping to establish an environment that supports healing, recovery and reconciliation.

Writing a letter is a participatory act that can be done at any time of the year, and ultimately supports the mission of Orange Shirt Day and the Orange Shirt Society.

DONATE

When you donate a monetary gift to the Society, your name will appear on their website as a contributor to the growth of Orange Shirt Day!

www.orangeshirtday.org

THE OFFICIAL SHIRT OF 2020

The official shirt of 2020 was created by grade 9 student Jackson Eiteneier of Calgary, Alberta.

"Orange Shirt Day is a way to show my culture as well as looking out for other youth in the world... My art represents the Divine protection of a mother or father of their child. In the larger hand there is designs which represent experience. In the child's hand there is only a little bit of design at the root of the hand, the rest being white. It's showing the protection of an elder for the child."

- Jackson Eiteneier [5]

CHAPTER SIX QUESTIONS

REVIEW

1. What does Orange Shirt Day have the power to do?
2. Are there any limits on how you can participate in Orange Shirt day?
3. Are you welcome to create your own Orange Shirt? If so, what does it need to include?
4. Is there an official orange shirt? What happens to a portion of the proceeds?
5. Regardless of where you get your orange shirt, what message should be on the shirt and what colour should it be?
6. What are some of the books available to learn about Phyllis's story?
7. How can you become an advocate for Orange Shirt Day?
8. Murray Sinclair said " _____ is the key to reconciliation… We need to look at the way we are educating _____. That's why we say that this is not an _____ problem. It's a _____ problem."
9. What are some of the options available to your school to participate?
10. What is unlearning?

ACTIVITY

Create an informational poster with resources:

Use your creativity to make it visually appealing!

Create a Poem using the word O.R.A.N.G.E.
Have each letter represent a word or sentence relating to Orange Shirt Day.

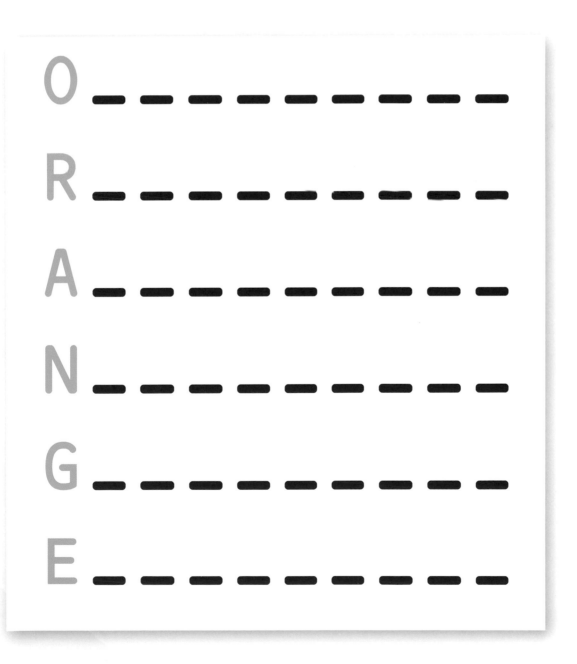

REFLECTION

1. What does "holding a space for Survivors and their families to share their experiences" mean? Why is this important in regards to the goals of Orange Shirt Day?

2. Your participation and education will also help you to confront racism, stereotypes and prejudices, against Indigenous people. In order to be effective at confronting racism, stereotypes and prejudices what do think that education needs to include?

3. What are territory acknowledgements and how do they relate to walking a path of reconciliation? What is your territory acknowledgment?

RESEARCH

Getting to know Indigenous resources in your community is critical to increasing your education. What are some Indigenous resources available to you and your school? You can create a list, a PowerPoint presentation, or a poster.

SOURCES

1. "The Orange Shirt Story: The True Story of Orange Shirt Day." Bookmanager. <https://bookmanager.com/tbm/?searchtype=keyword&qs=the+orange+shirt+story&qs_file=&q=h.tviewer&using_sb=status&qsb=keyword> accessed September 30, 2018.
2. "Top BC Best Sellers Published in 2019." Read Local BC. January 8, 2020. <https://www.readlocalbc.ca/2020/01/08/top-20-bc-bestsellers-published-in-2019/> accessed May 24, 2020.
3. "Orange Shirt Society." Orange Shirt Day. <https://www.orangeshirtday.org/orange_shirt_society.html> accessed May 1, 2020.

   Webstad, Phyllis. Personal Interview. January. 2020.
4. "Truth and Reconciliation Chair Urges Canada to Adopt UN Declaration on Indigenous Peoples." CBC News. Haydn Watters. June 1, 2015. <https://www.cbc.ca/1.3096225?__vfz=medium%3Dsharebar> accessed May 15, 2020.
5. Eiteneier, Jackson. Personal Interview. May. 2020.

Medicine hearts filled with traditional medicines including tobacco, cedar, sweet grass and sage. Photo courtesy of Jacqueline Maurer and the Dze L K'ant Friendship Centre on the Wet'suwet'en Territory

CHAPTER

7 RECONCILIATION
BUILDING A FUTURE TOGETHER

The Orange Shirt Society is always exploring and striving to have a greater understanding of reconciliation and what it means for Canadians. The Society's first purpose is "to support Indian Residential School Reconciliation."

During the course of researching and interviewing people for this book, it became apparent that there are many views of reconciliation and that they are all valid. A person's view of reconciliation will depend on their experiences, cultural heritage, upbringing, education, and where they live. When combined, this makes up their **worldview**.

Oxford dictionary defines worldview as:
"A largely unconscious but generally coherent set of presuppositions and beliefs that every person has which shape how we make sense of the world and everything in it. This in turn influences such things as how we see ourselves as individuals, how we interpret our role in society, how we deal with social issues, and what we regard as truth." [1]

The Orange Shirt Society decided to present some of those views and challenge you, the reader, to figure out what reconciliation means to you. As you walk your personal journey of reconciliation the Society also challenges you to participate in discussions and think about how it affects your classmates, school, families and communities.

There is no right and wrong way to explore reconciliation.

In 2014, the Assembly of First Nation's Chiefs in Council passed a resolution supporting Orange Shirt Day stating "Call upon all Canadians to listen with open hearts to the stories of survivors and those affected by Residential School to fully comprehend each other. This is a first step in reconciliation." [2]

In this chapter, the Society has heavily quoted from the Truth and Reconciliation Commission's (TRC) final report issued in June, 2015, which is available in its entirety at www.trc.ca. The final report ends with 94 Calls to Action stating, "in order to redress the legacy of Residential Schools and advance the process of Canadian reconciliation...". [3] They are directed at governments, schools, businesses, and all Canadians, and they call on all of us to implement change.

Children marching for Orange Shirt Day in Shulus, B.C. Photo taken by Dara Hill of the Merritt Herald.

Artwork by Fern Hill School student Sabriyya Ashe

WHAT ARE PEOPLE SAYING ABOUT RECONCILIATION?

There are many facets of reconciliation in Canada that people are engaged in. The Orange Shirt Society focuses on Indian Residential School Reconciliation which also includes the process and the personal journey. In this context, reconciliation is new and people are still trying to understand and trust it.

Reconciliation in the Oxford English Dictionary is defined as:

"an end to a disagreement or conflict with somebody and the start of a good relationship…". [

Anne Burrill, one of the founders of Orange Shirt Day, said, *"reconciliation is both a personal journey and a public process."* [5]

The Truth and Reconciliation Commission described reconciliation as *"an ongoing individual and collective process, and will require commitment from all those affected including First Nations, Inuit and Métis former Indian Residential School students, their families, communities, religious entities, former school employees, government and the people of Canada. Reconciliation may occur between any of the above groups."* [6]

The Truth and Reconciliation Commission stated, *"reconciliation is about establishing... a respectful relationship between Aboriginal and non-Aboriginal peoples in this country. For that to happen, there has to be awareness of the past, acknowledgement of the harm that has been inflicted, atonement for the causes, and action to change behaviour".* [7]

Elder Stephen Augustine said, *"...there is both a place for talking about reconciliation and a need for quiet reflection. Reconciliation cannot occur without listening, contemplation, meditation, and deeper internal deliberation."* [8]

British Columbia Premier John Horgan said, *"Reconciliation is hard work. It does not begin or end with a single decision, event or moment. No single one of us decides what reconciliation can or should look like. It is a shared journey we are on together. We know that this work isn't easy. If we're going to achieve it, we have to stay committed to this process, keep engaging with one another and find common ground."* [9]

As a founding member of the Reconciliation Canada initiative and a generous supporter of the Orange Shirt Society, Vancity states that:

"The reconciliation process is important for all Canadians because it's about the basics of how we treat each other as fellow human beings and the kind of relationships and communities we want to build for the future...

For many Canadians we don't really know much about the ongoing impact of Indian Residential Schools—how it continues to be felt throughout generations and contribute to social problems... More than 150,000 First Nations, Métis, and Inuit children were placed in these schools. Connections with culture and family, parenting skills, and intergenerational relationships were damaged or lost. People were broken. It's time to acknowledge and understand the past, and find a new way forward." [10]

Lorena Fontaine, a participant in an Aboriginal Women's digital storytelling project on intergenerational reconciliation, said, *"reconciliation is about stories and our ability to tell stories. I think the intellectual part of ourselves wants to start looking for words to define reconciliation. And then there is the heart knowledge that comes from our life experiences. It's challenging to connect the two and relate it to reconciliation..."* [11]

Chief Fred Robbins says, *"the monuments [that were erected in the SJM commemoration] were intended for people, to reconcile the spirits of Residential School Survivors and provide freedom to be themselves as triumphant First Nations people. During the reunion, I felt First Nations being heard by mainstream society for the first time in Williams Lake. For the first time, non-First Nations people were aware of the Residential School. In general, reconciliation is recognizing that something happened, that healing needs to happen, otherwise it can still happen."* [12]

Chief Fred Robbins with one of two commemorative monuments. Photo by Monica Lamb-Yorski of the Williams Lake Tribune.

THE RECONCILIATION PROCESS

Through the making of this book, there were three themes that were undeniably evident as prerequisites for reconciliation in Canada. These three themes are education, truth telling, and recognizing our shared history.

EDUCATION

The cornerstone of reconciliation is education. Many Indigenous leaders, including Murray Sinclair, Chief Fred Robbins and Phyllis Webstad, have discussed the critical importance of education moving forward with reconciliation in Canada.

Senator and TRC chair Murray Sinclair stated that *"seven Generations of children went through the Residential Schools. Each of those children who were educated were told that their lives were not as good as the non-Aboriginal people of this country. They were told that their languages and their culture were irrelevant... As a result, many generations of children, including you and your parents, have been raised to think about things in a different way… in a way that is negative when it comes to Aboriginal people. We need to change that. It is the educational system that has contributed to this problem in this country and it is the educational system that, we believe, will help us get away from this. We need to look at the way we educate children. We need to look at the way we educate ourselves. We need to look at what our textbooks say about Aboriginal people. We need to look at what it is Aboriginal people themselves are allowed to say within the educational systems about their own histories... Because it took us so many generations to get to this point it's going to take us at least a few generations to say that we are making progress. We cannot look for quick and easy solutions, because there are none. We need to be able to look at this from the perspective of where do we want to be in three, four, five or seven generations from now when we talk about the relationship between Aboriginal and non-Aboriginal people in this country. If we can agree on what that relationship needs to look like in the future, then what we need to think about is what can we do today that will contribute to that objective. Reconciliation will be about ensuring that everything we are doing today is aimed at that high standard of restoring that balance to that relationship."* [13]

Senator Murray Sinclair, as the Chief Commissioner for the Truth and Reconciliation Commission, said, *"…as a commission we have said we have to start addressing the way we teach our children about Aboriginal people. We have to address how we teach our children about Canadian history so that they can grow up understanding that things are not as rosy as some schools have been teaching them. We have to teach them properly about the invalidity of the* **doctrine of discovery**.*"* [14]

Chief Fred Robbins' story offers perspective of lack of education around the existence of Residential Schools.
"I rode with a prominent member of the School District to a soccer tournament once, and they asked about my childhood. To my surprise they had no clue that there was a Residential School here. Also Kerry Cook (former mayor of Williams Lake) told me that her knowledge of the Residential School was the pool she used to swim in. We weren't allowed to swim in it. And, when I revisited the 150 Mile Elementary School (where I attended class when I lived at the Residential School), where my old classmate was now principal, he didn't know that I went 'home' each night to the horrors of the Residential School." [15]

The TRC Final Report states that, *"…all students – Aboriginal and non-Aboriginal – need to learn that the history of this country did not begin with the arrival of Jacques Cartier on the banks of the St. Lawrence River. They need to learn about the Indigenous Nations the Europeans met, about their rich linguistic and cultural heritage, …"* [16]

TRUTH TELLING

In order to achieve reconciliation every person must make the effort to listen to the painful truths of what took place in Residential Schools as well as the intergenerational impacts. Orange Shirt Day opens the door to conversations of all aspects of Residential School and provides a safe place for Survivors and their families to tell their truths.

Phyllis Webstad says that *"the truth of what happened needs to be told and understood in order for Reconciliation to happen. I, as a Survivor, call upon all Canadians to open their minds and hearts to hear our truths."* [17]

Kerry Cook, the mayor of Williams Lake during the time of the commemoration project events, and current Orange Shirt Society Board member, reflected on her relationship with Chief Fred Robbins. She said, *"I remember his courage for speaking his truth. His strength and vulnerability came from somewhere deep inside of him and as he shared his story it stirred or awakened something deep inside of me. It is not very often that you experience a divine encounter; a shared vision that awakens your very soul. Looking back it was as though the soil of my heart had been prepared for this very moment. When he shared his vision it was as though he was planting a seed deep into my heart."* [18]

OUR SHARED HISTORY

The painful history of Indian Residential Schools belongs to all Canadians. Now it is every Canadian's responsibility to learn about the past and make informed choices in the present moment that create an inclusive future.

Phyllis Webstad stated *"this isn't just Indigenous history, this is Canadian history."* [19]

Murray Sinclair declares that *"reconciliation overall, from the commission's perspective, means that we also have to convince Canadian society that this is their story as well."* [20]

The Truth and Reconciliation Commission's final report shares one non-Indigenous woman's experience. She said, *"by listening to your story, my story can change. By listening to your story, I can change."* [21]

RECONCILIATION IS THE FUTURE

The movement of Orange Shirt Day has shown us that people, especially Canada's youth, are committed to creating a bright future in which reconciliation is a way of life.

Chief Fred Robbins feels that, *"reconciliation must happen in due course. You can't put a timeline on it. Once reconciliation is accomplished at some level, there needs to be restitution, giving us back our authority, it has to be different."* [22]

Phyllis Webstad passionately states that her objective is *"to keep telling my story so that people in the world will know first hand what has gone on and that it will never be repeated. For my grandchildren, that they will live different and better lives and the lives of future generations will increasingly improve in this new world we create. We are all here, no one is going away. We need to learn to live together, and to respect each other."* [23]

Elder Barney Williams, member of the Truth and Reconciliation Commission's Survivor Committee, said, *"I think more and more people are realizing that the engagement of youth is crucial. For me, as a Survivor, I'm really impressed with how much they knew. I was very impressed with the type of questions the audience asked. It tells me, as somebody who's carried this pain for over sixty-eight years, that there's hope. Finally there's hope on the horizon and it's coming from the right place. It's coming from the youth."* [24]

Murray Sinclair declared, *"I really don't care if you feel responsible for the past. The real question is do you feel a sense of responsibility for the future because that's what this is all about."* [25]

Phyllis also said, *"I read recently that reconciliation is dead. When I read that I thought no it isn't! The seed of reconciliation is being planted in elementary and high schools across Canada".* [26]

When discussing the future, Murray Sinclair said,
"...reconciliation isn't going to come easily, it took us 150 years of these schools to create this damage. You know, my grandfather was a carpenter and he used to tell me, 'It's a lot easier to knock something down than it is to build it.' They [the Canadian Government] spent 150 years knocking things down, so it may take us that long to build it back up again. But, we have to build it up...We have to learn how to get along and we have to learn how to get along respectfully." [27]

"Our future, and the well-being of all our children rests with the kind of relationships we build today" **says Chief Dr. Robert Joseph. O.B.C. a Residential School Survivor and founder of Reconciliation Canada.** [28]

The artwork that children created using Orange Shirt Day and reconciliation as their inspiration shows us that Phyllis and Elder Barney Williams are correct. Canada's youth are more passionate than ever about restoring Indigenous rights and revealing their collective truths. This artwork, also shows us that the education system in Canada is beginning to change and that truthful Indigenous history is being discussed and taught in the classroom.

RECONCILIATION AND THE PATH FORWARD

Whatever your path to reconciliation looks like, keep forging ahead. The journey may not be easy at times, but your contributions are guaranteed to change the future. Remember that you are not on this journey alone. Phyllis Webstad, the Orange Shirt Society and many other people are walking this path with you. Actions taken and commitments made today will affect future generations of Canadians.

The Truth and Reconciliation Commission final report states that, *"All Canadians must make a firm and lasting commitment to reconciliation in order to ensure that Canada is a country where our children and grandchildren can thrive."* [29]

When asked if he had any advice for non-Indigenous Canadians, Chief Fred Robbins had this to say: *"Spread the word. Stay the path. Know that you're not just helping yourself to learn and understand, you're helping generations of Residential School Survivors. The term **"ally"**, comrade-in-arms, means that you understand although you haven't lived it so you can't fully, and you want to make it better. When speaking from the heart, there is no way to lose if coming from the heart, no right or wrong."* [30]

At Queen's University, in their Faculty of Law building, there is a powerful Murray Sinclair quote that reads, *"the road we travel is equal in importance to the destination we seek. There are no shortcuts. When it comes to truth and reconciliation we are forced to go the distance."* [31]

Phyllis Webstad signs a student made blanket at Chester Area Middle School on January 27, 2019 in Nova Scotia. Photo by Sarah Philbrick.

The last word is from Phyllis Webstad:

"During my time presenting to schools and organizations across Canada, I met some astounding and amazing people of all ages and races. What I witnessed first-hand is that people care, that they want to hear our truths, and that they are committed to the process of reconciliation. When people know better, they can do better. When I get a chance to speak to Survivors directly, I'm always sure to tell them about this and how I believe that our future is in good hands. One day there will be no survivors left in Canada, and I want other Survivors to know we can leave this earth knowing that the children are learning about what happened to us and they empathize, and they will make sure it never happens again." [32]

CHAPTER SEVEN QUESTIONS

REVIEW

1. What makes up one's worldview?
2. Is there a right or wrong answer when it comes to understanding reconciliation?
3. How does the Oxford dictionary define reconciliation?
4. How does the Truth and Reconciliation Commission of Canada define reconciliation?
5. Fill in the blanks. Anne Burrill stated "reconciliation is both a _____ journey and a _____ process."
6. Fill in the blanks. BC Premiere John Horgan stated "reconciliation is _____ work. It does not begin or end with a _____ decision, event or moment. No single one of us decides what reconciliation can or should look like. It is a _____ journey."
7. What is considered to be the cornerstone of reconciliation?

ACTIVITY

Make a collection of reconciliation quotes from your classroom and/or school. Have each student write their view of reconciliation on a small piece of paper cut out like an orange shirt that can be put together in a book or on display.

REFLECTION

1. What does Reconciliation mean to you? What are some actions that you are able to take to participate in the process?

2. Residential Schools were in operation for over one hundred years and impacts are still felt today. What do you think Reconciliation will look like in the next hundred years? How will the lives of Indigenous people be different?

3. Find an example of someone in this book or beyond that demonstrated walking the path to reconciliation. What did they do? What inspired them? What impact did they have?

RESEARCH

Now that you have learned a lot about reconciliation and Orange Shirt Day, imagine you are in charge of hosting an Orange Shirt Day event.
Write up a day plan with details about your event including the following:

- What will people do?
- How will you advertise the event?
- How will you engage people in conversations about Residential Schools?
- Who would you invite to the event?
- How do you host an Elder at your event with respect and generosity?

Refer to www.orangeshirtday.org for more resources and ideas.

SOURCES

1. "Worldview." Oxford Reference. <https://www.oxfordreference.com/view/10.1093/oi/authority.20110803124830471> accessed May 15, 2020.

2. "Assembly of First Nations 2014 General Assembly, Halifax, N.S." <https://www.afn.ca/uploads/files/afn_aga_2014_resolutions_final_en.pdf> accessed May 25, 2020. pp. 18.

3. "Truth and Reconciliation Commission of Canada: Calls to Action." Truth and Reconciliation Commission of Canada. 2015.<http://trc.ca/assets/pdf/Calls_to_Action_English2.pdf> accessed February 1, 2020.

4. "Reconciliation." Oxford Learner's Dictionaries. <https://www.oxfordlearnersdictionaries.com/definition/english/reconciliation> accessed May 25, 2020.

5. "Artist Workshops to Focus on Reconciliation." The Williams Lake Tribune. <https://www.wltribune.com/community/artist-workshops-to-focus-on-reconciliation/> accessed May 24, 2020

6. "Our Mandate." Truth and Reconciliation Commission of Canada. <http://www.trc.ca/about-us/our-mandate.html> accessed April 20, 2020.

7. "Canada's Residential Schools: Reconciliation. The Final Report of the Truth and Reconciliation Commission of Canada. Volume 6." Truth and Reconciliation Commission of Canada. McGill-Queen's University Press, Montreal & Kingston, London, Chicago. 2015. <http://www.trc.ca/assets/pdf/Volume_6_Reconciliation_English_Web.pdf> accessed May 24, 2020. pp. 3.

8. "Honoring the Truth, Reconciling for the Future. Summary of the Final Report of Truth and Reconciliation Commission of Canada." Truth and Reconciliation Commission of Canada. 2015. <http://www.trc.ca/assets/pdf/Honouring_the_Truth_Reconciling_for_the_Future_July_23_2015.pdf> accessed pp. 17.

9. "Victoria Police Investigating Reports of Assault at Wet'suwet'en Protect at BC Legislature." Chek News. Julian Kolsut and Tess Straaten. Vancouver. Febuary 11, 2020. <https://www.cheknews.ca/protests-continue-in-victoria-ahead-of-throne-speech-645602/> accessed May 24, 2020.

10. "Reconciliation Canada." Vancity. <https://www.vancity.com/AboutVancity/InvestingInCommunities/Partnerships/ReconciliationCanada/> accessed May 24, 2020.

11. "Honouring the Truth, Reconciling for the Future. Summary of the Final Report of Truth and Reconciliation Commission of Canada." Truth and Reconciliation Commission of Canada. 2015. <http://www.trc.ca/assets/pdf/Honouring_the_Truth_Reconciling_for_the_Future_July_23_2015.pdf> accessed on May 20, 2020. pp. 242.

12. Robbins, Chief Fred. Personal Interview. February. 2020.

13 "Justice and Federal Commissioner Murray Sinclair Speech." Truth and Reconciliation Commission. The Commemoration Project Events. Filmed by John Dell. Signal Point Media, 2013. DVD.

14. "Justice and Federal Commissioner Murray Sinclair Speech." Truth and Reconciliation Commission. The Commemoration Project Events. Filmed by John Dell. Signal Point Media, 2013. DVD.

15. Robbins, Chief Fred. Personal Interview. February. 2020.

16. "Canada's Residential Schools: Reconciliation. The Final Report of the Truth and Reconciliation Commission of Canada. Volume 6." Truth and Reconciliation Commission of Canada. 2015. McGill-Queen's University Press, Montreal & Kingston, London, Chicago. <http://www.trc.ca/assets/pdf/Volume_6_Reconciliation_English_Web.pdf> accessed May 24, 2020. pp. 119.

17. Webstad, Phyllis. Personal Interview. January. 2020

18. Cook, Kerry. Personal Interview. March. 2020.

19 Webstad, Phyllis. Personal Interview. January. 2020.

20. "Justice and Federal Commissioner Murray Sinclair Speech." Truth and Reconciliation Commission. The Commemoration Project Events. Filmed by John Dell. Signal Point Media, 2013. DVD.

21. "Final Report of the Truth and Reconciliation Commission of Canada, Volume 1." Truth and Reconciliation Canada. <http://www.trc.ca/assets/pdf/Volume_1_History_Part_1_English_Web.pdf> accessed May 2, 2020. pp. 21.

22. Robbins, Chief Fred. Personal Interview. Febuary. 2020.

23. Webstad, Phyllis. Personal Interview. January. 2020.

24. "Honouring the Truth, Reconciling for the Future. Summary of the Final Report of Truth and Reconciliation Commission of Canada." Truth and Reconciliation Commission of Canada. 2015. <http://www.trc.ca/assets/pdf/Honouring_the_Truth_Reconciling_for_the_Future_July_23_2015.pdf> accessed on May 20, 2020. pp. 243.

25. "Justice and Federal Commissioner Murray Sinclair Speech." Truth and Reconciliation Commission. The Commemoration Project Events. Filmed by John Dell. Signal Point Media, 2013. DVD.

26. Webstad, Phyllis. Personal Interview. January. 2020.

27. "Justice and Federal Commissioner Murray Sinclair Speech. "Truth and Reconciliation Commission. The Commemoration Project Events. Filmed by John Dell. Signal Point Media, 2013. DVD.

28. "Reconciliation Canada." <https://reconciliationcanada.ca/> accessed on May 25, 2020.

29. "Honouring the Truth, Reconciling for the Future. Summary of the Final Report of Truth and Reconciliation Commission of Canada." Truth and Reconciliation Commission of Canada. 2015. <http://www.trc.ca/assets/pdf/Honouring_the_Truth_Reconciling_for_the_Future_July_23_2015.pdf> accessed on May 20, 2020. pp. 317.

30. Robbins, Chief Fred. Personal Interview. Febuary. 2020.

31. "Keeping reconciliation at the forefront." Queen's Gazette. September 12, 2019. <https://www.queensu.ca/gazette/stories/keeping-reconciliation-forefront> accessed May 25, 2020.

32. Webstad, Phyllis. Personal Interview. January. 2020.

CHAPTER 8 ARTWORK
CANADIAN STUDENTS' REFLECTIONS

In 2019, the Orange Shirt Society along with publisher Medicine Wheel Education created an art contest that saw hundreds of students from around Canada submitting their artwork and creative writing using Orange Shirt Day as their inspiration. The selected submissions were to be featured in this book. This project allowed for students to have artistic freedom and express themselves in whatever way they wanted. The submissions gave an inside look into the way young people are processing the historical truths and traumas of Indian Residential Schools.

The Orange Shirt Day artwork that was received, and has been seen online, reflects social change, social justice, human rights and personal reconciliation. These submissions showed that young people are truth seekers, using their creative brains to uncover a painful past and empathize with Residential School Survivors, their families, and those who didn't come home. The artwork and writing has displayed the many ways that young people are trying to understand Residential School information and reconciliation.

The young people used this project to express a variety of emotions, thoughts and actions. Some greatly empathized with the experiences of Phyllis, other Survivors and people they know; others discussed how sad it would be for them if they had to leave their families. Many addressed their own action plans to create a new legacy for Indigenous peoples and more shared their strong opinions on what they want the future of Canada to look like. A majority of the submissions displayed an incredible knowledge of Indigenous traditions, showing that a cultural resurgence is underway. Additionally, a lot of submissions highlighted the fact that every child deserves to be safe at school and that attempting to remove a person's identity and individuality is wrong. Overall, the submissions strongly exhibited that Canada's youth are dedicated to creating social change and healing for both Survivors and themselves.

ARTWORK AND WRITING THEMES

As submissions were reviewed, several themes emerged. The participants used this opportunity to inspire, educate, challenge, heal and share personal stories in a variety of ways. They used colour, graphics, words, and textures to express sentiments such as empathy, sorrow, anger, gratitude, connection, motivation and ambition.

One theme that was evident in every submission was that each demonstrated empathy for Residential School Survivors and respect for Indigenous cultures.

A school wide art project called the 'Bricks of Belonging Wall' by Maple Creek Public School. Photo courtesy of teacher Heather Brandes.

WRITING SUBMISSIONS

Grade 7 student Sara Gacesa, from Ontario's Maple Creek Public School, shows her vision as well as the energy surrounding a Residential School.

"It wasn't until this year that I fully understood what truly happened to those children who attended Residential Schools. Before doing my artwork, I had to do my research and what I found shocked me. Around 150,000 children attended Residential Schools, and over 6,000 died. Many of them never received a proper burial, and this is why my artwork is to raise awareness of this matter. The children who attended Residential Schools have suffered, and those who live to tell the tale are very courageous, strong and have incredible endurance to persevere through all those tough times. I will always respectfully acknowledge the idea that every child matters... I think people should understand that Canada was not always the land it is now and it has a very dark history. Every Child Matters, and no matter what religion, gender, ethnicity, and culture or race we are all equal and all deserve to have the same rights and opportunities. Nobody, especially a child should ever feel alone or discriminated against because of who they are. For over 130 years, the motto for Residential Schools was "take the Indian out of the child," children died from smallpox, while others were listed as "missing" or "discharged." In some cases, parents never found out what happened. I think the most important thing that everybody should learn is to be proud of who they are, and to never forget their roots and where they come from. Don't let others change you."

Grade 7 student Sara Gacesa, from Ontario's Maple Creek Public School.

Some writing submissions discussed how Residential Schools affected them personally as Intergenerational Survivors or as Indigenous people. For example, Grade 7 student Shirel Matagne Bogne from Harold Peterson Middle School in New Brunswick wrote this moving poem:

"I am Wolastoqiyik

I am proud of who I am

I am proud of my skin color and religion

No amount of soap, scrubbing or bleach will remove the Indian in me

No amount of chores, beating or punishment would make me forget who I am

I am proud of who I am

I am Wolastoqiyik"

- Grade 7 student Shirel Matagne Bogne

As someone whos never faced discrimination based on my skin tone and history, its hard to fully understand how this must feel for Indignous people. I've never had to go through this sort of suffering before but people of my colour have inflicted this pain on people countless times. It's important to me that we end the cycle of suffering for these people though I think many of these people will never get to feel free of those feelings and it upsets me that I can't do anything about that. But, growing up as someone whos part of the LGBT+ community, I'm understand why they would not be able to forgive and move on and I'm not bothered by them feeling this way as we cannot fix all the suffering that has happened or will continue to happen. We can only truely teach love and acceptace to ourselves for the future.

Grade 11 student Lauren Giesbrecht writes about her thoughts on Orange Shirt Day and Residential Schools.

DEAR PHYLLIS... DEAR SURVIVOR...

The artists and writers often wrote *"Dear Phyllis"* or *"Dear Survivor"* on their creations showing that they used empathy as a way to connect with Survivors and the traumas caused by Residential Schools.

Dear Phyllis.
Sorry about your experience, but its over... woohoo! Did you hear about kids killing themselves? Sounds sad but its true... well I'm Stetson, I'm Indigenous too! You inspired me to stand up for Indigenous people. This is how you inspired me by saying in the book that natives were treated poorly, but we should be treated equally.

BY Stetson

Every Child Matters

Orange Shirt

Name: Stetson   Grade: 4\5

"Every Child Matters"

A letter to Phyllis Webstad written by grade 4/5 student Stetson Wilson-Chayer.

Dear Phyllis:

I felt super sad about you and the other children who went to residential schools. I felt so heartbroken, I can't even imagine this all happening to me. I am so unbelievably sorry that you weren't able to wear your orange shirt on your first day of school. They took away your individually. Just remember every child matters.

Sincerly,
Jaya Saroya

A letter to Phyllis Webstad written by Grade 10 student Jaya Saroya.

ELLINGTON
MONTESSORI

40 Cowdray Court
Toronto, ON M1S 1A1
Tel: 416.759.8363

admin@ellingtonmontessori.ca
www.ellingtonmontessori.ca
www.facebook.com/EllingtonMontessoriSchool
www.twitter.com/EllingtonCanada

Dear Ms. Webstad,

Ms Webstad, it is a privilege to be writing to you. I have learned about Orange Day during the classroom discussion about the residential schools and that encouraged me to know more about your story. I was overwhelmed to find out what you went through at St. Joseph Mission Residential School. Ms. Webstad, it must have been hard to be living in such a traumatic state of mind, at such a young age.

I think the era of residential schooling was one of the darkest spans of Canadian history. It must have been an awful experience when the young children were deprived of being with their families, following their tradition and even something as basic as eating what they like. My heart goes out to all the 150, 000 students at residential schools at that time who were abused physically, mentally and emotionally. It must have been an unimaginable extent of suffering.

This year, in my school, the elementary students performed a skit. The skit revolved around the incident when your grandma hands over an orange shirt to you and how brutally it was taken away. While we were playing the characters it felt like we were living those moments ourselves. On the other hand, we have been fortunate enough to have one of the residential school survivors among us as a guest of honour. She was in tears throughout our performance. Later, Elder Chaboyer began to share her own experience of the residential school she went to and it left us speechless.

The story of suppression does not end here. Unfortunately, it still continues when a child is bullied, when one is taken for granted, when one is not treated well, when one is made to feel unworthy, it is very disheartening to go through these emotions especially as a child.

However, there is always a light at the end of the tunnel. Ms. Webstad, I have learnt a lot through your story. You inspire me to be patient through the tough times and face the rainy days. Also it made me realize we, as children, are privileged to be living with our families, go to a school that we like, to be able to play and talk with our friends and more such; things in our lives we are grateful for. Thank you for choosing to share your story that in a way has been a catalyst to encourage the younger generation.

Yours sincerely,

Josephine, Somasundaram

Grade – five

A letter to Phyllis Webstad written by grade 5 student Josephine Somasundaram from Ellington Montessori School.

WHAT RESIDENTIAL SCHOOLS LOOKED LIKE

Another theme displayed within the art pieces was the chilling visualization of how young people see Residential Schools based on the dark history and Survivor's stories.

Orange Shirt Day artwork by grade 11 student Mikayla Schreiner.

Artwork by grade 7 student Ethan Kong.

Orange Shirt Day inspired artwork by grade 7 student Noor Bajwa.

IDENTITIES BEING TAKEN AWAY

Young people connected with the pain and anguish Phyllis Webstad and other Survivors felt as their individuality was taken from them at Residential School.

Artwork by grade 12 student Lauren Nichols.

CREATING A NEW INCLUSIVE CANADA FOR INDIGENOUS PEOPLE

Many of the submissions depicted a vision for a more inclusive and safe Canada. One student redesigned the Canadian flag.

Artwork by Fern Hill School student Sabriyya Ashe

Artist Sabriyya Ashe reimagined the Canadian flag to be inclusive of Indigenous cultures. She wrote, *"this is how I think the Canadian flag should be. As most people know, the red of the Canadian flag is meant to represent Britain and the white is meant to represent France; however, somehow the First Nations peoples were forgotten in making the flag we know today. I redesigned the flag trying to represent the First nations people of Canada. I used motifs and art specific to certain regions across the country. The top strip represents the Inuit, the right strip represents the Woodlands people, the bottom strip represents the Plains groups, and the left strip represents the North West Coast nations. I added the symbol of the Métis flag as well as an Inukshuk and a feather to represent all three First Nations people in this country."*

BEFORE AND AFTER RESIDENTIAL SCHOOL

Artwork using a split vision to depict emotions before and after Residential School were common among the submissions.

Every Child matters

Artwork by grade 10 student Ava Scully showing a child's appearance before and after Residential School.

AWARENESS OF INDIGENOUS TRADITIONS AND SYMBOLS

Many students showcased their knowledge of Indigenous cultures, traditions and symbols through their artwork and writing submissions.

Artwork by grade 7 student Malcolm Atkins.

Artwork by grade 5 student Halleluya Gifford.

Artwork by grade 10 student Jocelyn Allen

EYES

Eyes were a powerful symbol used throughout the submissions. The eyes were used to show the emotional turmoil that Residential Schools have caused.

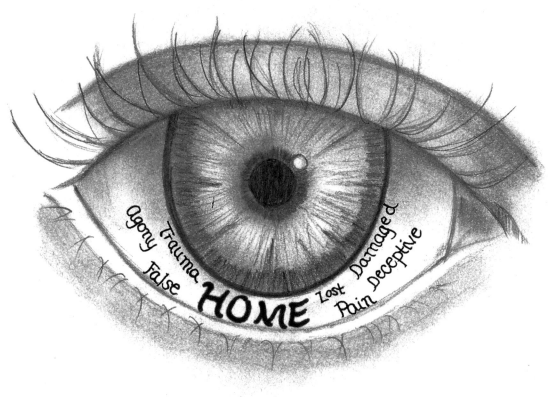

Artwork by grade 11 student Juliana Tajan.

Artwork by grade 11 student Alyssa Sawan.

COLLECTIVE PROJECTS

Many schools and classes worked together to create larger than life art pieces. Nearly all of these projects were put together using smaller individual artwork to create larger collective pieces.

A school-wide art project called the 'Bricks of Belonging Wall' by Maple Creek Public school. *"This Bricks of Belonging Wall mural represents Maple Creek Public Schools' commitment to reconciliation in Canada. It was a school-wide Orange Shirt Day initiative from October 2019, that acknowledges the horrifying and traumatic effects of the Residential School system on Indigenous Peoples and was created by sharing and learning the truth about our collective history. As a school, we continue to educate ourselves about the long lasting impact of these schools and are dedicated to learning about Indigenous Peoples both past and present through building relationships. Encouraging children to feel proud and comfortable with their identities is integral to their well being and school is a place where we strongly believe they must feel that they matter and belong."* Photo courtesy of teacher Heather Brandes.

A collective artwork by Mme Carmen Bellehumeir's 2019 grade 2 class at École Arthur Pechey Public School. Student artists are Max, Kovian, Olivia, Lily, Ryder, Aimeree, Seth, Rylee, Evan, Nirvana, Alexis, Makenna, Ivy, Kozik, Jamie.

ORANGE SHIRTS

Dozens of submissions depicted personalized versions of the orange shirt. Artists used either the template that was offered or created their own version. Many shirts included depictions of Phyllis Webstad, St. Joseph's Residential School, Indigenous symbols and of course the words, "Every Child Matters."

Valleyview secondary school September 2019 Orange Shirt Day Secwépemctsin Class.

Artwork by grade 6 student Alexandre Coté.

Artwork by grade 7 student Abby Billard.

A collective patchwork artwork made by teacher Julie Rempel's grade 5/6 class at William Mason School.

Grade 9 student Gianna Pellerin's Orange Shirt Day artwork.

HOW DOES WEARING AN ORANGE SHIRT CREATE CHANGE?

Some of the submitted writing pieces asked tough and unexpected questions, which showed young people's commitment to creating change for Survivors and their families. Some wondered how wearing an orange shirt creates change or what the future of Orange Shirt Day will look like.

Orange Shirt Day has created a platform for education based on both historical facts and Survivor stories. Wearing an orange shirt on September 30th generates more awareness and opportunities for reconciliation. As you think about buying or making your orange shirt, you will inevitably become educated on Phyllis Webstad's story. Your education will allow you to inspire the next person who asks, "Why are you wearing an orange shirt?"

Orange Shirt Day inspires the initiative to create powerful social change, justice and reconciliation throughout the entire year. It takes time to create change, and September 30th acts as the beginning of a profound journey for many.

All of the artwork, photos and quotes in this chapter were submitted to Medicine Wheel Education through a Canada-wide art contest in the fall of 2019. Medicine Wheel Education was given written permission from each student and student's parent/guardian to use their artwork and/or writing submissions in this book.

Every Child Matters!

Student artwork by Hartlee Rempel

9 GLOSSARY

Allyship or being an ally is the process of building long-lasting relationships based on trust and respect.

Assimilation is the process of a minority cultural group being absorbed into a more dominant society resulting in the loss of culture, language, and knowledge.

A **band**, "or 'Indian Band,' is a governing unit of Indians in Canada instituted by the Indian Act, 1876. The Indian Act defines a 'band' as a 'body of Indians.'" [1]

Children who didn't come home from Residential Schools because they died, from malnutrition, disease or injuries due to the circumstances and abuses endured at the schools. Many children also attempted to run away from the Residential Schools, but they died trying to find their way home. Records show that 6000 children died in Residential Schools, but records are incomplete and it is believed that far more children didn't come home. [2]

Colonization occurs when settlers attempt to take over a foreign land by forcefully imposing their own politics and culture.

Doctrine of Discovery is the ideology that North America was "discovered" by Europeans. "The Doctrine of Discovery was used by European monarchies, beginning in the mid-fifteenth century, as a means of legitimizing the colonization of lands outside of Europe" by considering the land vacant or uninhabited. Even though Indigenous people were already living on these lands they were considered by Europeans to be non-human, thus justifying the "discovery." [3]

(Chief) **Fred Robbins** is Northern Secwépemc (Shuswap) from Esk'etemc First Nation (Alkali Lake). Chief Fred Robbins has a vision for reconciliation which involved all people remembering and learning what happened at St. Joseph's Mission Residential School, honouring and helping the Survivors recover from their experience and ultimately reconciling together.

First Nations "is a term used to describe Aboriginal peoples of Canada who are ethnically neither Métis nor Inuit." [4]

Genocide "means any of the following acts committed with intent to destroy, in whole or in part, a national, ethnical, racial or religious group, as such: Killing members of the group; Causing serious bodily or mental harm to members of the group; Deliberately inflicting on the group conditions of life calculated to bring about its physical destruction in whole or in part; Imposing measures intended to prevent births within the group; Forcibly transferring children of the group to another group." [5]

Indian is an erroneous and outdated term used to describe Indigenous People. It is based on the mistaken assumption by early European explorers that they had arrived in India. Unfortunately, it is still a 'legal' term employed within the 1876 Indian Act, which is still in use. Today 'Indian' is a derogatory term, and it will only be used in this book when referring to Indian Residential Schools and other legal terms within the Indian Act. [6]

The **Indian Act** is a Canadian federal law enacted in 1876 that allowed the government the regimented management of Indigenous peoples and their lands. The purpose of the Indian Act was to control, marginalize and oppress Indigenous people. [7]

An **Indian agent** was an administrator or representative for the Canadian government who had authority over Indigenous people and reserve lands. [8] As Phyllis Webstad explained "The Indian Agent had more power than the Chiefs and the Matriarchs." [9]

Indian Residential Schools (also referred to as Industrial schools)
"Residential Schools for Aboriginal people in Canada date back to the 1870s. Over 130 Residential Schools were located across the country, and the last school closed in 1996. These government-funded, church-run schools were set up to eliminate parental involvement in the intellectual, cultural, and spiritual development of Aboriginal children. During this era, more than 150,000 First Nations, Métis, and Inuit children were placed in these schools often against their parents' wishes. [10] Many were forbidden to speak their language and practice their own culture. While there is an estimated 80,000 former students living today, the ongoing impact of Residential Schools has been felt throughout generations and has contributed to social problems that continue to exist." The TRC only referred to Canadian government run schools. There were other Residential Schools and Day Schools across the country as early as 1620, run by churches and other organizations. [11]

Indian Residential School Reconciliation is an on going collective process that involves both Indigenous and non-Indigenous Canadians bravely acknowledging, and educating each other, on the mistreatment of Indigenous peoples through the Residential School system. Reconciliation aims to create a new legacy for Indigenous Canadians that supports a healing journey and sees a respectful resurgence of cultural traditions.

Indigenous, or, **Aboriginal**, people, "are the descendants of the original inhabitants of North America. The Canadian Constitution recognizes three groups of Aboriginal people - Indians, Métis and Inuit. These are three separate peoples with unique heritages, languages, cultural practices and spiritual beliefs." [12]

Intergenerational Survivor "refers to an individual who has been affected by the intergenerational dysfunction created by the experience of attending Residential School." [13]

Intergenerational Trauma is the transmission of historical oppression and its negative consequences across generations. [14]

John A MacDonald was the first prime minster of Canada. It was his government's decision to open three schools, in 1883, off reserve through government funding that marked "the beginning of Canada's Residential School System." [15]

Inuit "Aboriginal people in Northern Canada, who live in Nunavut, Northwest Territories, Northern Quebec and Northern Labrador. The word means 'people' in the Inuit language —Inuktitut. The singular of Inuit is Inuk." [16]

Métis People are "...mixed First Nation and European ancestry who identify themselves as Métis, as distinct from First Nations people, Inuit or non-Aboriginal people." [17]

A **national trauma** occurs when a traumatic event or experience effects a collective group of people across a country. Indian Residential Schools have resulted in a national trauma.

Orange Shirt Day occurs annually on September 30 and honours the Indigenous children who attended Indian Residential Schools, their families and the children who didn't come home. Orange Shirt Day encourages the education and awareness of Indian Residential School Reconciliation and proudly declares that 'Every Child Matters.'

The **Orange Shirt Society** is a non-profit organization, whose purposes are to promote Indian Residential School reconciliation, to raise awareness of the impacts of Indian Residential Schools, and their continuing intergenerational impacts, and to promote the concept of "Every Child Matters."

Phyllis Jack Webstad is a Residential School Survivor from the Stswecem'c Xgat'tem (Canoe Creek/Dog Creek) First Nation in British Columbia. In 2013, Phyllis inspired the Orange Shirt Day movement by sharing the story of losing her shiny orange shirt on her first day of school at the St. Joseph Mission Residential School.

Racism is the discrimination against someone who is of a different race based on the belief that one race is superior to another.

Reconciliation - See Chapter 7

Reserves "An area of land set aside by the federal government for the use and occupancy of a First Nations group or band.." [18]

Resilience is having the ability to sustain and recover from trauma and challenges.

St. Joseph's Mission Residential School was located just outside of Williams Lake, B.C. It opened in 1872 and closed in 1981. St. Joseph's Mission Residential School has also been called The Mission, Williams Lake Indian School, Williams Lake Industrial School, Cariboo Residential Industrial School and Cariboo Student Residence. [19]

Survivors are Indigenous people who attended Residential Schools and survived the experience, as some did not. The TRC estimated that as many as 6000 children died in the Residential Schools or as a result of the schools. [20]

The Truth and Reconciliation Commission (TRC) of Canada was founded on June 2nd, 2008 and aimed to reveal truths of Residential Schools and provide support for Survivor and their families. The TRC was created out of the Indian Residential School Settlement Agreement (IRSSA). [21]

Unlearning is the process of discarding or overriding learned habits, lessons and concepts.

The City of **Williams Lake** lies within the Cariboo Regional District of British Columbia and is situated on the traditional territory of the T'exelcemc (Williams Lake Band), members of the Secwépemc Nation (Shuswap People). [22]

Worldview: A largely unconscious but generally coherent set of presuppositions and beliefs that every person has which shape how we make sense of the world and everything in it. This in turn influences such things as how we see ourselves as individuals, how we interpret our role in society, how we deal with social issues, and what we regard as truth. [23]

SOURCES

1. "Bands." Indigenous Foundations UBC Arts. <https://indigenousfoundations.arts.ubc.ca/bands/> accessed May 25, 2020.
2. "Truth and Reconciliation Commission: By the Numbers." CBC News. Daniel Schwartz. June 3, 2015. <https://www.cbc.ca/news/indigenous/truth-and-reconciliation-commission-by-the-numbers-1.3096185> accessed May 1, 2020.

   "Residential Schools Findings Point to 'Cultural Genocide,' Commission Chair Says." CBC News. John Paul Tasker. May 15, 2015. <https://www.cbc.ca/news/politics/residential-schools-findings-point-to-cultural-genocide-commission-chair-says-1.3093580> accessed March 30, 2020.
3. "Christopher Columbus and the Doctrine of Discovery: 5 Things to Know." Indigenous Corporate Training. October 3, 2016. <https://www.ictinc.ca/blog/christopher-columbus-and-the-doctrine-of-discovery-5-things-to-know> accessed by May 25, 2020.
4. "Terminology." Indigenous Foundations UBC Arts. <https://indigenousfoundations.arts.ubc.ca/terminology/#firstnations> accessed May 1, 2020.
5. "Genocide." United Nations Office on Genocide Prevention and the Responsibility to Protect. <https://www.un.org/en/genocideprevention/genocide.shtml> accessed February 15, 2020.
6. "Indian." The Canadian Encyclopedia. May 11, 2020. <https://thecanadianencyclopedia.ca/en/article/indian-term> accessed May 15, 2020.
7. The Truth and Reconciliation Commission of Canada. They Came for the Children. Manitoba: Library and Archives Canada Cataloguing in Publication, 2012. pp. 11.
8. "Indian Agents in Canada." The Canadian Encyclopedia. October 25, 2018. <https://www.thecanadianencyclopedia.ca/en/article/indian-agents-in-canada> Accessed May 28, 2020.
9. Webstad, Phyllis. Personal Interview. January. 2020.
10. "Residential School." Truth and Reconciliation Commission. <http://www.trc.ca/about-us.html> accessed October 15, 2020.
11. The Truth and Reconciliation Commission of Canada. They Came for the Children. Manitoba: Library and Archives Canada Cataloguing in Publication, 2012. pp. 5.
12. "Archived - Common Terminology." Indigenous and Northern Affairs Canada. March 11, 2013. <https://www.aadnc-aandc.gc.ca/eng/1358879361384/1358879407462> accessed May 1, 2020.
13. "Intergenerational survivors." Where are the Children. November 28, 2013. <http://wherearethechildren.ca/en/watc_blackboard/intergenerational-survivors/> accessed May 10, 2020.
14. "Intergenerational Survivors." Where are the Children. November 28, 2013. <http://wherearethechildren.ca/en/watc_blackboard/intergenerational-survivors/> accessed May 10, 2020.

    "The Intergenerational Trauma of First Nations Still Run Deep." The Global and Mail. Berube, Kevin. February 16, 2015. <https://www.theglobeandmail.com/life/health-and-fitness/health-advisor/the-intergenerational-trauma-of-first-nations-still-runs-deep/article23013789/> accessed May 24, 2020.
15. The Truth and Reconciliation Commission of Canada. They Came for the Children. Manitoba: Library and Archives Canada Cataloguing in Publication, 2012. pp. 5.
16. "Archived - Common Terminology." Indigenous and Northern Affairs Canada. March 11, 2013. <https://www.aadnc-aandc.gc.ca/eng/1358879361384/1358879407462> accessed May 1, 2020.
17. "Archived - Common Terminology." Indigenous and Northern Affairs Canada. March 11, 2013. <https://www.aadnc-aandc.gc.ca/eng/1358879361384/1358879407462> accessed May 1, 2020.
18. "On-Reserve First Nations Communities: Canada Pandemic Influenza Preparedness: Planning Guidance for the Health Sector." Government of Canada. December 5, 2017. <https://www.canada.ca/en/public-health/services/flu-influenza/canadian-pandemic-influenza-preparedness-planning-guidance-health-sector/influenza-pandemic-planning-considerations-in-on-reserve-first-nations-communities.html> accessed February 15, 2020.
19. Tarbell, Harold. St. Joseph's Mission Residential School Commemoration Project Document. Remembering, Recovering, and Reconciling. Williams Lake: Tarbell Facilitation Network, 2013.
20. "Residential Schools Findings Point to 'Cultural Genocide,' Commission Chair Says." CBC News. John Paul Tasker. May 15, 2015. <https://www.cbc.ca/news/politics/residential-schools-findings-point-to-cultural-genocide-commission-chair-says-1.3093580> accessed March 30, 2020.
21. "About the National Centre for Truth and Reconciliation." National Centre of Truth and Reconciliation. University of Mantioba. <http://nctr.ca/about-new.php> accessed May 15, 2020.
22. Williams Lake Band. <https://williamslakeband.ca/> accessed April 30, 2020.
23. "Worldview." Oxford Reference. <https://www.oxfordreference.com/view/10.1093/oi/authority.20110803124830471> accessed May 15, 2020.